OPEN THE EYES OF
MY HEART

INTEGRITY
PUBLISHERS

Open the Eyes of My Heart

Devotions copyright © 2002, Integrity Publishers. Written by Debbie Carsten.

Published by Integrity Publishers, a division of Integrity Media, Inc., 5250 Virginia Way, Suite 110, Brentwood, TN, 37027.

Produced with the assistance of The Livingstone Corporation. Project staff includes David Veerman, Neil Wilson, Linda Taylor, Ashley Taylor.

Interior design/Cover design by The Office of Bill Chiaravalle | www.officeofbc.com.

ISBN 1-59145-021-7

Printed in the United States of America

02 03 04 05 06 RRD 5 4 3 2 1

TABLE OF CONTENTS

INTRODUCTION

The glorious songs for worship that we know and love come from God's own divine hand. He is the Master Composer. He created music. He inspires it. He desires its sweet aroma to drift up to him from his people. God *dwells* in the joy and praises of his people.

Music is an intimate and personal way for all believers to approach the glistening throne of God and bow our hearts humbly before him. It's one of the extraordinary ways he has made it possible for us to communicate to him our love, our joy, our gratitude, our eternal faith and devotion.

Open the Eyes of My Heart is a majestic and moving daily devotional based on a collection of the most powerful praise and worship songs of all time. The lyrics alone will lift your spirits, express for you the feelings you may have difficulty expressing, and allow you to experience God's saving grace and amazing love.

Why not spend a few minutes alone with God each day by focusing on one of these magnificent songs written to glorify and honor him? Sing the song of praise, read God's Word, pray reverently to him. Then rejoice as God responds in love to your worship by opening the eyes of your heart to wonders and glories he alone can reveal. That devoted time will undoubtedly be the most exceptional moments of your day.

May God bless you as you come to him with a willing spirit and a moldable mind, that he may lift you up and shape you into all you are meant to become.

OPEN THE EYES
OF MY HEART

Open the eyes of my heart, Lord,
Open the eyes of my heart,
I want to see You, I want to see You.
Open the eyes of my heart, Lord,
Open the eyes of my heart,
I want to see You, I want to see You.

To see You high and lifted up,
Shining in the light of Your glory,
Pour out Your pow'r and love
As we sing holy, holy, holy.

Holy, holy, holy,
Holy, holy, holy,
Holy, holy, holy,
I want to see You.

—PAUL BALOCHE

Our vision may be 20/20, but how well do we see with the "eyes of our hearts"? We cannot see Jesus with our physical eyes; it takes special eyes—the eyes of our hearts—to be able to see Jesus, high and lifted up, shining in all of His glory and holiness. Such words well up from the bottom of our souls: Open the eyes of my heart, Lord; I want to see You.

Jesus is at work; we just don't see it sometimes because His ways are so different from ours. Who would plan to birth the King of kings and Lord of lords in a stable, to a peasant girl? Alone and destitute, Mary could have doubted that she was seeing Jesus. Maybe it was her willingness to be so humbled and still believe that made her the best servant for the awesome task to which God called her.

You are seeing with the eyes of your heart when you hold on despite what your eyes can see. When God takes you through an all-time low, will you stay confident in His ability to still work through you?

I pray also that the eyes of your heart may be enlightened in order that you may know the hope to which he has called you, the riches of his glorious inheritance in the saints, and his incomparably great power for us who believe.

EPHESIANS 1:18, 19a

PRAYER

Unless we remind ourselves of the truth, we slip into believing only what we can see. Confess what you believe about Jesus. For example: "Jesus, I believe You are at work in my life. I believe You have every situation under control. I believe You want to work through me for Your glory."

C ELEBRATE   J ESUS

Celebrate Jesus, celebrate!
Celebrate Jesus, celebrate!
He is risen. He is risen,
And He lives forevermore.
He is risen. He is risen.
Come on and celebrate
The resurrection of our Lord.

—GARY OLIVER

The most exciting three words in the English language are "He is risen." The angel beside Jesus' open tomb spoke these words to the women who had come to anoint Jesus' dead body. The angel asked them why they were looking in a grave for someone who was alive. Jesus was no longer there! He is alive! He is risen! He lives forevermore.

Surely those three days while Jesus lay in the tomb were filled with darkness. Jesus had died, and along with Him seemed to go the dreams and hopes of so many. The women who came to anoint His body surely believed that the story was over. Perhaps a few of Jesus' followers remembered His words, "Three days later [I] will rise" (Mark 10:34). But most seem to have missed it somehow.

When Jesus arrived among His followers after His resurrection, they were filled with joy! Can you picture it? We serve a Savior who died and rose again. Because He lives, we, too, will live forever. Join in! Come on and celebrate the resurrection of our Lord!

He is not here; he has risen, just as he said. Come and see the place where he lay.

MATTHEW 28:6

PRAYER

Meditate on the awesome promise of living forever with Jesus. Talk to the Lord about how He wants you to be prepared to be with Him forevermore.

THIS IS THE DAY

This is the day
That the Lord has made.
I will rejoice
And be glad in it.
O this is the day
That the Lord has made.
I will rejoice
And be glad in it.

—AUTHOR UNKNOWN

Scripture is always prompting us to embrace today. *"Now* is the day of salvation" (2 Corinthians 6:2); "Today, if you hear his voice, do not harden your hearts" (Hebrews 3:15). God knows we can only live in the present, and He encourages us to make good use of it.

This day is our gift from God. We can waste it with regrets over our past or worries about our future. We can squander it trying to outrun yesterday's miseries. We can ignore it, lost in our wishful thinking. It's up to us to decide what to do with it. God would have us make the most of this day. What are you seeking for tomorrow? More opportunities? Better relationships? Personal growth? Embrace today. Learn the lessons the Lord requires of you today. Be faithful with the things God entrusts you with today. Let God's presence sustain you through this day's trials. Rejoice in the opportunities God brings to you today.

God has a future for you, but you have to live in today to get there. Step out in faith when God asks you to trust Him. This is the day that the Lord has made. Rejoice and be glad!

This is the day the LORD has made; let us rejoice and be glad in it.

PSALM 118:24

PRAYER

Ask Jesus to help you trust the past and the future into His hands. Affirm that He will lead you into His future for you and prepare you for it, as you are faithful today. Then listen to what He has called you to do today.

I WILL CELEBRATE

I will celebrate, sing unto the Lord,
Sing to the Lord a new song.
I will celebrate, sing unto the Lord,
Sing to the Lord a new song.

With my heart rejoicing within,
With my mind focused on Him,
With my hands raised to the heavens,
All I am, worshiping Him.

—PAUL AND RITA BALOCHE

When God gets hold of us, He doesn't just give us a makeover on the outside. He changes us from the inside out. He makes us brand-new people. When Jesus comes into our lives, "the old has gone, the new has come" (2 Corinthians 5:17b).

So what is the "old" that God replaces with the "new"? Our hearts that once were cold and closed are replaced with new hearts that beat in tune with His—hearts that rejoice from within. Our minds that once were controlled by the lies and fears of Satan are transformed to think like Christ—minds that focus on God. Our hands that worked to please ourselves are transformed into instruments of worship—hands raised to heaven in praise through our work.

This gives us the "new song" we sing. Our new song comes from a rejoicing heart, a focused mind, and serving hands. With every fiber of our being, all that we are, we worship the Lord. Now that's a real celebration!

I will sprinkle clean water on you, and you will be clean; I will cleanse you from all your impurities and from all your idols. I will give you a new heart and put a new spirit in you; I will remove from you your heart of stone and give you a heart of flesh.

 E Z E K I E L   3 6 : 2 5 ,   2 6

P R A Y E R

As you pray, ask God to take His place at the very center of your life. Ask the Lord to show you how to revolve your heart, mind, and hands around Him and His plans.

H E   I S   E X A L T E D

He is exalted; the King is exalted on high,
I will praise Him.
He is exalted, forever exalted,
And I will praise His name.
He is the Lord,
Forever His truth shall reign.
Heaven and earth,
Rejoice in His holy name.
He is exalted; the King is exalted on high.

—TWILA PARIS

These moving words remind us that God rules. He is exalted on high; forever His truth shall reign. Even as we rejoice, so heaven and earth rejoice with us in our King's holy name.

When life hands us situations that we don't understand, we can remember that our King reigns. He is the Lord. When we sorrow over the shortness of life, we can remember that our King is forever. When we worry about what lies surround us, we can remember that our King's truth shall reign. When we tremble at the evil in the world, we can remember that our King's name is holy.

Nothing that happens is beyond our King's control. Nothing surprises Him. Unlike any human king or leader, God is incorruptible, unchangeable, and eternal. He is worthy of our exaltation. He deserves our highest praise. Heaven and earth are rejoicing in His holy name. As Jesus said, even "if they keep quiet, the stones will cry out" (Luke 19:40). There's a chorus being sung in all of creation. We can sing along, exalting our King!

Yours, O LORD, is the greatness and the power and the glory and the majesty and the splendor, for everything in heaven and earth is yours. Yours, O LORD, is the kingdom; you are exalted as head over all.

1 CHRONICLES 29:11

PRAYER

Spend some time just exalting and praising God. Rejoice in His holy and eternal name.

BLESSED BE THE LORD
GOD ALMIGHTY

Father in Heaven, how we love You,
We lift Your name in all the earth.
May Your kingdom be established in our
praises,
As Your people declare Your mighty works.

Blessed be the Lord God Almighty,
Who was and is and is to come.
Blessed be the Lord God Almighty,
Who reigns forevermore.

—BOB FITTS

ow we love you, Father in heaven. How we praise you for all your mighty works." We sing the words, but how often do we truly think of God's mighty works on our behalf? Do our friends and family know what God has done for us? When was the last time we declared His mighty works?

Psalm 106 describes how the Israelites repeatedly forgot about God's many kindnesses to them in the desert. When they stopped remembering God's greatness, however, they started relying on themselves. They rebelled against God. Life became all about their rules and plans and happiness—with devastating results.

We can learn from the Israelites. Declaring God's mighty works and praising Him every day will help keep our lives on track and inspire hope in the people who hear us. Join in the chorus of praise to our Lord God Almighty who reigns forevermore! When people see what God can do in an ordinary life, they just might open the window wider to God's possibilities for them. Maybe they will even see ways that God is already at work in their lives. Then they, too, can praise Him and declare His mighty works for all to hear!

Great is the LORD and most worthy of praise; his greatness no one can fathom. One generation will commend your works to another; they will tell of your mighty acts. They will speak of the glorious splendor of your majesty, and I will meditate on your wonderful works.

PSALM 145:3-5

PRAYER

Reflect on the past twenty-four hours with a thankful heart. Don't neglect the small things God has done. Sometimes it's the little things that show us how carefully we're loved.

L O R D ,   I   L I F T   Y O U R   N A M E   O N   H I G H

Lord, I lift Your name on high,

Lord, I love to sing Your praises,

I'm so glad You're in my life,

I'm so glad You came to save us.

You came from heaven to earth

to show the way,

From the earth to the cross, my debt to pay,

From the cross to the grave,

from the grave to the sky

Lord I lift Your name on high.

—RICK FOUNDS

Lord, I lift Your name on high, I love to sing Your praises!" What joyous words of adoration to our Lord! The Lord loves to hear us sing. He loves to hear our voices raised in praise as we thank Him for coming into our lives, as we thank Him for saving us.

The words to this song are the gospel in a nutshell. Jesus came from the glories of heaven down to this earth. The Bible tells us He left paradise to come to this tiny planet all because of His great love for us. We were lost, and He came to show us the way—the path to follow to find salvation. He came as a human so that He could die as a human on the cross and pay our debt—the death penalty our sins deserved. Through His death, we are set free from our sin and from eternal death. But Jesus did not stay dead. He rose again and returned to heaven with the promise that one day we will join Him there. He came, He died, He paid our debt, and He calls the whole world to come to Him.

No wonder we lift His name on high!

Therefore I will praise you among the nations, O LORD; I will sing praises to your name.

PSALM 18:49

PRAYER

Thank the Lord for the awesome privilege to sing His praises! Thank Him for giving you something to sing about—His presence in your life, His salvation, His payment of your debt in full.

I   E X A L T   T H E E

I exalt thee, I exalt thee,
I exalt thee, O Lord.
I exalt thee, I exalt thee,
I exalt thee, O Lord.

For Thou, O Lord, are high above
all the earth,
Thou art exalted far above all gods.
For Thou, O Lord, art high above
all the earth,
Thou art exalted far above all gods.

—PETE SANCHEZ, JR.

Something about beholding vast beauty draws us in. Whether it's an endless sky or a rolling ocean, our spirits are refreshed in the presence of greatness. We're wired to revel in it. We want to drink it in.

God knows how much we need this experience, so He invites us time and again to come to Him—the greatest One of all. His hands spread out the heavens. His authority set the stars in place. No beauty or majesty on earth can compare to His.

Yet often we miss it because the worries of life crowd God out. When the pressure is on, we are tempted to want everyone and everything to revolve around us—our tight schedule, many demands, and important agendas. It takes God-given willpower to make Him our focus. Yet when we do, our spirits are refreshed by His greatness. When we exalt our awesome God who is "high above all the earth," we place our focus where it belongs—on Him.

Praise the LORD, O my soul. O LORD my God, you are very great; you are clothed with splendor and majesty. He wraps himself in light as with a garment; he stretches out the heavens like a tent . . . He set the earth on its foundations; it can never be moved.

PSALM 104:1-2, 5

PRAYER

Ask God to reveal more of His beauty to you today. Then look for the ways He will answer.

S H I N E ,   J E S U S ,   S H I N E

Shine, Jesus, shine!
Fill this land with the Father's glory.
Blaze, Spirit, blaze!
Set our hearts on fire.
Flow river flow—
Flood the nations with grace and mercy
Send forth Your Word, Lord,
And let there be light.

Lord, the light of Your love is shining,
In the midst of the darkness shining,
Jesus, light of the world, shine upon us,
Set us free by the truth You now bring us,
Shine on me, shine on me.

Lord, I come to Your awesome presence,
From the shadows into Your radiance,
By the blood I may enter Your brightness,
Search me, try me, consume all my darkness,
Shine on me. Shine on me.

—GRAHAM KENDRICK

A s Christians who pray, "Your Kingdom come," we long to see our homes, neighborhoods, and workplaces filled with Jesus' light. The words of this uplifting song explain how this can happen.

The more time we spend in God's awesome presence, the more we become changed into His likeness. Every minute that we spend gazing into His face, the more He will consume our darkness so that our faces can display His glory. Because we tend to become like those with whom we spend time, why not spend some time lingering in God's presence today? Imagine His perfect ways that can weave together a good plan for your life. Listen to His gracious and forgiving words as you confess your failures. Soak in His relentless tenderness as you give Him your burdens. Gaze on His kingly brightness so that your face can display His likeness. The more you spend time with Him, the more you will be changed. Then so will your world.

And we, who with unveiled faces all reflect the Lord's glory, are being transformed into his likeness with ever-increasing glory, which comes from the Lord, who is the Spirit.

2 CORINTHIANS 3:18

PRAYER

Thank the Lord for allowing you into His awesome presence. Ask Him to make your face display His likeness. Ask that your life will tell His story—the story of salvation through Him.

THERE IS A REDEEMER

There is a Redeemer,
Jesus, God's own Son,
Precious Lamb of God,
Messiah, Holy One.

Jesus, my Redeemer,
Name above all names,
Precious Lamb of God,
Messiah, O for sinners slain.

Thank You, O my Father
For giving us Your Son
And leaving us Your Spirit
'Til the work on earth is done.

—KEITH GREEN

God deserves our most heartfelt thanks. This song provides the opportunity to express our profound gratitude to God for sending Jesus to us. He didn't have to. He could have let us live aimless, worthless lives, eventually dying far from Him. He didn't have to love us; He didn't have to save us. After all, our sin had hurt Him deeply and separated us from Him eternally.

God knew we were lost. He knew we were hopeless and that the only way to save us would be to do it Himself. So He did that, coming to earth in His Son.

Then, when Jesus returned to heaven, He gave us His Holy Spirit. Jesus called Him our "Counselor" who would be with us forever (John 14:16). God did not leave us to our own devices; He left us the Holy Spirit to walk with us and to guide us.

The Holy Spirit empowers us to do Christ's work on earth—the work of serving, loving, sharing, and helping others enter the kingdom. One day God's work on earth will be done. On that day, we will rejoice at all that God has done in us and through us for His glory!

And I will ask the Father, and he will give you another Counselor to be with you forever —the Spirit of truth. The world cannot accept him, because it neither sees him nor knows him. But you know him, for he lives with you and will be in you.

JOHN 14:16, 17

PRAYER

Thank God for giving His Son for you. Thank Him for the presence of His Holy Spirit in your life who helps you live for Him.

SHOUT TO THE LORD (I)

My Jesus, my Savior, Lord, there is none like You.
All of my days I want to praise the wonders of
Your mighty love.
My comfort, my shelter, tower of refuge and
strength,
Let every breath, all that I am, never cease to
worship You.

Shout to the Lord all the earth; let us sing!
Power and majesty, praise to the King!
Mountains bow down and the seas will roar
At the sound of Your name.
I sing for joy at the work of Your hands.
Forever I'll love You, forever I'll stand.
Nothing compares to the promise I have in You.

—DARLENE ZSCHECH

This song moves us because it combines the two essentials of great worship. First, it encourages our utmost abandonment. Words like "every breath," "all that I am," and "never cease," declare complete devotion. Our hearts never truly engage in worship so long as we hold anything back.

Matthew 28:17 tells of Jesus appearing to His eleven disciples after His resurrection. "When they saw him, they worshiped him; but some doubted." Clearly two camps of people stood in Jesus' presence: the worshipers and the doubters. Maybe the doubters held back because they feared what Jesus might do. Just recently they had relied on Him, only to find their world shattered by a crucifixion. We are just as vulnerable to disappointment. Christians aren't spared from pain, sorrow, and trials. But we can know God's love as greater and so abandon ourselves into His care. When doubts hold us back, we miss the life-changing power of worship.

Second, this song inspires great worship because it raises Jesus to the highest place. All power and majesty belong to Him. Even inanimate objects have the good sense to bow at the sound of His name. Nothing exists that isn't subject to His authority. Yet, this same Jesus is so intimate and personal that we dare to call Him "my Jesus," "my Savior." Truly no one else is like Him.

My lips will shout for joy when I sing praise to you—I, whom you have redeemed.

PSALM 71:23

PRAYER

Ask God, who gave Himself completely for you, to help you give yourself completely to Him.

S H O U T   T O   T H E   L O R D   (2)

My Jesus, my Savior, Lord there is none like You.
All of my days I want to praise the wonders of
Your mighty love.
My comfort, my shelter, tower of refuge and
strength,
Let every breath, all that I am, never cease to
worship You.

Shout to the Lord all the earth; let us sing!
Power and majesty, praise to the King!
Mountains bow down and the seas will roar
At the sound of Your name.
I sing for joy at the work of Your hands.
Forever I'll love You, forever I'll stand.
Nothing compares to the promise I have in You.

—DARLENE ZSCHECH

The psalms are filled with exhortations to "shout" and "rejoice," to praise God enthusiastically. At times, however, we sure don't feel like praising God, and certainly not aloud. Loss and pain push us from Him, causing us to focus on our hurts and tears. Doubt, fear, and defeat also become enemies of joy, bringing with them an almost suffocating cloud of depression.

At these times, we need to raise our heads and look again at who God is and what He has done for us. As this powerful song reminds us, He is our Savior, comfort, shelter, refuge, and strength. Surely no one compares to our powerful and loving God.

What is stealing your joy? Bring it to the Lord and then thank Him for being with you and working in you. Remember who He is, what He has done, and what He has promised. Your praise may start as a whisper, but keep praising. Soon you will be singing and shouting for joy! Nothing can compare to the promises we have in Him!

Rejoice in the LORD and be glad, you righteous; sing, all you who are upright in heart!

PSALM 32:11

PRAYER

Spend five minutes praising God in prayer. Don't ask for anything; simply thank Him for who He is and for His work in the world and in your life.

I C O U L D   S I N G   O F   Y O U R   L O V E   F O R E V E R

Over the mountains and the sea,

Your river runs with love for me.

And I will open up my heart,

And let the Healer set me free.

I'm happy to be in the truth,

And I will daily lift my hands.

For I will always sing

Of when Your love came down.

I could sing of Your love forever.

I could sing of Your love forever.

I could sing of Your love forever.

I could sing of Your love forever.

—MARTIN SMITH

This wonderful song compares God's love to a river. Like a surging river, God's love flows into our lives. Over the difficulties and through the trials, it penetrates every part of our souls. Nothing can stop its flow. It is at once the most powerful force and the most intimate truth we will ever know.

The question is, will we receive it? Will we open our hearts and let the Healer in? Will we bare our souls to Him and be so bold as to rely on Him? Will we let Him wash away our sins and shame? The river of His love is always giving, always available.

Expectations of how life should go, feelings of unworthiness, and giving in to self-pity can block the love God wants us to know. When we relinquish our attempts to control how and when God's love should come to us, we open ourselves to a flood. Today, you can let God be God and do what He does best—love you! Open your heart to receive the river of His love—and be ready for a swim!

They feast on the abundance of your house; you give them drink from your river of delights.

PSALM 36:8

PRAYER

Personalize and pray Paul's prayer from Ephesians 3:17b–19, "I pray that you, being rooted and established in love, may have power, together with all the saints, to grasp how wide and long and high and deep is the love of Christ, and to know this love that surpasses knowledge—that you may be filled to the measure of all the fullness of God."

THY WORD

I will not forget Your love for me, and yet
My heart forever is wandering.
Jesus be my guide, hold me to Your side,
And I will love You to the end.

Thy Word is a lamp unto my feet
And a light unto my path.
Thy Word is a lamp unto my feet
And a light unto my path.

—AMY GRANT AND MICHAEL W. SMITH

How feeble we are at following Christ. We love Him so much, we do not for a moment forget His love for us, and yet our hearts forever are wandering. We need Jesus to guide us, to hold us close by His side, to keep us on the right path.

Where can we meet Jesus, our Guide? In the pages of His Word. His Word is a lamp, like a bright flashlight, for our feet, giving us enough light for the next step on the path. God's Word provides direction for our lives. We may not always get the clear answer we want, but as we read about men and women like us, we'll be encouraged at what God can do through ordinary people, and our faith in God's possibilities will grow. The Bible has a way of examining our motives, too, so we can see more clearly what is God's leading and what's just our own thinking.

We can take comfort in knowing that God desires to guide us and is actively seeking to teach us to follow Him. We overcome our fear to step out when we rely on God's ability to find us and bring us back if we lose our way. Our decisions are messy and imperfect at best, but His hold on us is infinitely reliable.

For the word of God is living and active. Sharper than any double-edge sword, it penetrates even to dividing soul and spirit, joints and marrow; it judges the thoughts and attitudes of the heart.
HEBREWS 4:12

PRAYER

Ask the Lord to use His Word to light up the path ahead and show you the way you should go.

A W E S O M E   G O D

Our God is an awesome God!
He reigns from heaven above
With wisdom, power and love.
Our God is an awesome God!

—RICH MULLINS

Saying that God is "awesome" means we recognize that He is awe-inspiring. To consider Him causes us to stop in our tracks and forget everything else. His awesomeness would be frightening if we did not know of His great love for us. When we take the time to meditate on God, we cannot help but be changed. God is indeed awesome! This song reminds us that life is all about God. Everything was created by Him and for Him. He reigns from heaven over all of this earth. And His reign is perfect and perfectly just—He reigns with wisdom, power, and love.

We can get so caught up in our day-to-day lives that it's easy to forget that life isn't all about us. Even our prayer times can get caught up in being self-centered as we list what we want God to change and jabber on with our requests. When this happens, we walk away empty and wonder why we don't see more of God in our lives.

This awesome God invites us to revolve our lives around Him. He calls us to live His purposes, to receive all we need from Him, and to share the concerns on His heart. Then His awesome presence will fill us and overflow to a needy world.

Who among the gods is like you, O LORD? Who is like you—majestic in holiness, awesome in glory, working wonders?

EXODUS 15:11

PRAYER

Amos 3:3 asks, "Do two walk together unless they have agreed to do so?" Have you agreed to let God be God? Is He "awesome" to you? Talk to Him about that.

WHAT A MIGHTY GOD WE SERVE

What a mighty God we serve!
What a mighty God we serve!
Angels bow before Him,
Heaven and earth adore Him.
What a mighty God we serve!

—AUTHOR UNKNOWN

The book of Revelation tells us about a future party—to which we are invited! Multitudes from every nation will rejoice before God's throne. Angels will fall before Him in worship. All of heaven and earth will celebrate God's ultimate victory. We can only imagine what it will be like to have no more tears or sorrow, all things made new, and a wedding feast prepared for us by God Himself.

God indeed is mighty. Do you believe it? Do you believe in His might to work on your behalf? Release your faith to believe in your mighty God. Then watch and see. You will soon find yourself joining Mary in saying, "The Mighty One has done great things for me—holy is his name" (Luke 1:49).

But there's more to it. Not only does God work mightily on our behalf, but He also works in and through us—even when we are weak, frail, and unsure of ourselves. His might, working through us, can accomplish anything. Ask God to go to work in and through you. Then you'll understand what the angel meant when he said, "Nothing is impossible with God" (Luke 1:37).

Therefore God exalted him to the highest place and gave him the name that is above every name, that at the name of Jesus every knee should bow, in heaven and on earth and under the earth.

PHILIPPIANS 2:9, 10

PRAYER

Ask God to work mightily on your behalf. Then ask Him to work mightily through you to help someone else. Remember, with Him nothing is impossible.

MY LIFE IS IN YOU, LORD

My life is in You, Lord;
My strength is in You, Lord;
My hope is in You, Lord,
In You, it's in You.

—DANIEL GARDNER

hat encouraging words these are! If the source of our life or strength or hope were anything less than the Lord, we would be bound to fail. Because our *life* is rooted in God, we are eternal. Our lives are given purpose and fulfillment when we acknowledge Him as our Source.

Because our *strength* comes from Him, we are unbeatable. We have strength to sustain us through times of pain, difficulty, and suffering. We are strong even when we feel weak. In fact, we are promised that God's strength is made perfect in our weakness (2 Corinthians 12:9).

And when our *hope* is in Him, we will never be disappointed. Is it a hope that promises to give us what we want? Hardly! Is it a hope that promises lives that are free of pain? No, it's better than either of these. It's a hope that one day we will be changed to be like Jesus. God's power, love, peace, and joy will fill us completely. Instead of just a taste of His life in us now and then, we'll know the eternal bliss of oneness with Him. The Holy Spirit that God gave us guarantees that this hope will happen.

In him was life, and that life was the light of men.

JOHN 1:4

PRAYER

Ask God to help you remember that everything comes from His hand. Your life, your strength, and your hope depend on Him and His grace toward you.

MIGHTY IS OUR GOD

Mighty is our God,
Mighty is our King,
Mighty is our Lord,
Ruler of everything.

His name is higher,
Higher than any other name.
His power is greater,
For He has created everything.

—EUGENE GRECO, GERRIT GUSTAFSON, AND DON MOEN

These can be challenging words to believe. If God is so mighty, why do children stray from the truth? Why do our loved ones still suffer from cancer? Why are families broken apart by divorce? Surely the Creator has the power and authority to change these situations.

God rarely tells us the reasons why He allows suffering. But He does ask us to trust Him even when we don't have any answers. These times test our faith in God's character. Will we still believe He is mighty and good when He doesn't do what we want?

Every now and then God's might brings healing and restoration to turn a situation around. At other times, if we are to see His power, we must stretch our faith to look outside our limited idea of what we think is best. Our mighty God may choose to sustain us through a trial or, perhaps, take a handful of dust from a bad situation and slowly create something good.

We will never be hopeless as long as we keep believing in the truth of God's character. When you can't see His mighty power at work, look to the cross and remember that what appears to be defeat may just be God preparing for an even bigger victory.

Mightier than the thunder of the great waters, mightier than the breakers of the sea—the
Lord on high is mighty.

PSALM 93:4

PRAYER

Are you facing a challenge today? God is mighty; His power is great. Ask God to walk with you through the difficulty and to reveal Himself through it.

HE HAS MADE ME GLAD

I will enter His gates
With thanksgiving in my heart;
I will enter His courts with praise.
I will say this is the day
That the Lord has made.
I will rejoice for He has made me glad.

He has made me glad;
He has made me glad;
I will rejoice for He has made me glad.
He has made me glad;
He has made me glad;
I will rejoice for He has made me glad.

—LEONA VON BRETHORST

Do you want to be glad? Some people don't. They think they're better off not believing that anything good will happen to them. Gladness, to them, is only foolishness. Their version of Christianity has all the appeal of lemonade without the sugar.

Other people don't know how to be glad. They've lived for so long feeling bad about themselves that they don't feel right unless something is wrong.

Gladness springs from a heart full of childlike faith in a loving heavenly Father. Glad Christians know that they are precious to God. They believe God wants to bless them and lead them into good plans for their lives. When life sours, glad Christians pray, "Lord, You knew about this rough spot and have a plan to get through it. Show me Your way."

Being glad is up to you. You can choose to surrender your worries and lay down your burdens. A life of fear leads to despair, but faith leads to gladness. What will you choose?

The psalm writer knew about this choice. That's why so often we read words like, "I will give thanks to the LORD . . . and will sing praise to the name of the LORD Most High" (Psalm 7:17). What will you choose today? Come to the Lord and let Him make you glad!

Surely you have granted him eternal blessings and made him glad with the joy of your presence. PSALM 21:6

PRAYER

Revise Psalm 100:4, 5 as your prayer: "Enter his gates with thanksgiving and his courts with praise; give thanks to him and praise his name. For the LORD is good and his love endures forever; his faithfulness continues through all generations."

I WILL CALL UPON THE LORD

I will call upon the Lord,

Who is worthy to be praised.

So shall I be saved from my enemies.

The Lord liveth and blessed be my Rock,

And let the God of my salvation be exalted.

—MICHAEL O'SHEILDS

L ife rarely goes as we've planned. If you're not living the life you thought you'd have, you have plenty of company. Life, it seems, is what happens when we had other things planned.

Such was the case with Asa, ancient king of Judah. A vast army took up battle positions against him. To his credit, Asa called on the Lord for help. Maybe he even sang a song like this one—for the Lord indeed saved him from his enemies.

When a friend shares bad news, or a job promotion passes you by, or your kids act like they hate each other, where do you turn for help? Turn first to God's throne and call upon Him. Our Savior stands there, interceding for us. He is always asking His Father for the strength and courage we need to find victory.

This requires that we stop focusing on our problems, trying to figure everything out, and thinking it's all up to us. When we call upon the Lord, He fights for us. He has the power to change circumstances, create new solutions, and sharpen our perspective. With our eyes off our problems, the battle is won. Then we can join the chorus and exalt the God of our salvation.

Then Asa called to the LORD his God and said, "LORD, there is no one like you to help the powerless against the mighty. Help us, O LORD our God, for we rely on you, and in your name we have come against this vast army. O LORD, you are our God; do not let man prevail against you."

2 CHRONICLES 14:11

PRAYER

Ask the Lord to help you call upon Him with your battles, your fears, and your worries. And trust Him for the victory.

P R A I S E   T H E   N A M E
O F   J E S U S

Praise the name of Jesus.

Praise the name of Jesus.

He's my rock, He's my fortress,

He's my deliverer,

In Him will I trust.

Praise the name of Jesus.

—ROY HICKS JR.

How we love to complicate life! We easily take on more commitments than we can handle and fill our calendars with more activities than we can fit in. Yet all the busyness leaves us empty. We long to find our place, where we belong. We want to know what we were made for and how we fit in to the big picture.

Our great God answers all of our questions and fills all of our emptiness. When we worship and praise Him, when we bow our hearts and knees before Him, we realize who He is and what He has done. He is our rock—solid, immovable. We can count on Him always to be there. He is our fortress—a place of refuge where we can run for safety, protection, and comfort. He is our deliverer—our help when all hope seems gone.

Jesus told his friend Martha, "You are worried and upset about many things, but only one thing is needed" (Luke 10:41, 42). That one thing is Jesus Himself, and a willingness to sit at his feet and listen to Him. Will you slow down today and make Jesus your one thing? Instead of a full agenda, you'll find a full life.

He is the Rock, his works are perfect, and all his ways are just. A faithful God who does no wrong, upright and just is he.

DEUTERONOMY 32:4

PRAYER

Thank God for inviting you, again, to leave the swirling chaos of life and find your focus at His feet. Lay aside your pressures and burdens and give Him your full attention. Ask Him to fill your heart and mind with Himself.

ALL HAIL KING JESUS

All hail King Jesus,
All hail Emmanuel,
King of kings,
Lord of lords,
Bright Morning Star.
Throughout all eternity,
I'm going to praise Him,
And forevermore
I will reign with Him.

—DAVID MOODY

We praise our Emmanuel, "God with us," for who He is and for what He has done for us. And we will sing throughout eternity, for we will reign with Him forever. As Paul wrote to Timothy, "Here is a trustworthy saying: If we died with him, we will also live with him; if we endure, we will also reign with him" (2 Timothy 2:11, 12).

Imagine eternity with Christ! Our lives on this earth are merely a blip compared to eternity. The hardships we face here are a moment in time, preparing us to reign with our Lord forever.

Paul knew that those who endured hardships for the gospel would one day reign with Christ, and so he encouraged Timothy to persevere. As a prisoner, in chains, Paul could have resented his limitations. Not only did he endure the hardship, he didn't allow it to stop him from fulfilling what God had called him to do. Paul redirected his energies into mentoring Timothy, trusting that God's plan was bigger than his circumstances. His faith in God fueled his endurance.

We can have this same faith, a faith that lifts us above complaining about our lives and helps us embrace the opportunities in front of us. We can endure hardships when we remember that eternity is just around the corner, and we will be reigning with our Lord forever.

He has made everything beautiful in its time. He has also set eternity in the hearts of men; yet they cannot fathom what God has done from beginning to end.

ECCLESIASTES 3:11

PRAYER

Thank God for the promise of eternity. Ask Him to prepare you for the glorious future with Him.

M A J E S T Y   (I)

Majesty, worship His majesty,
Unto Jesus be all glory, honor and praise.
Majesty, kingdom authority,
Flow from His throne
Unto His own,
His anthem raise.

—JACK HAYFORD

Jesus has all authority in heaven and on earth. He is King of kings and Lord of lords. Worshiping his majesty means that we acknowledge His sovereign power and authority over us. His authority does not make us fearful; instead, it brings us peace because we know that He guides and protects us every step of our lives.

Jesus also gave authority to His followers. So He commissioned His disciples to go and change the world. They wouldn't be doing it in their own power! The good news of the gospel is that God can now live in us, giving us the power to do His work.

This power flows from Jesus' throne to us. When we acknowledge Jesus as our Lord, we can say, "The one who is in [us] is greater than the one who is in the world" (1 John 4:4). We have authority over darkness because the power of Jesus' light is in us. We have authority over lies because the Spirit of truth lives in us. We have power over bitterness and resentment because the God of all mercies lives in us.

We have victory in Jesus if we'll just live out what we've been given. It's not a victory to live the way we want to, but to live the way God wants us to. When we do that, we show His majesty and power to the world.

To him who is able to keep you from falling and to present you before his glorious presence without fault and with great joy—to the only God our Savior be glory, majesty, power and authority, through Jesus Christ our Lord, before all ages, now and forevermore! Amen.

JUDE 24, 25

PRAYER

Ask God how He might want to build His kingdom through you today. Believe that He will give you the power to do what He asks.

M A J E S T Y   (2)

Majesty, worship His majesty,
Unto Jesus be all glory, honor and praise.
Majesty, kingdom authority,
Flow from His throne
Unto His own,
His anthem raise.

—JACK HAYFORD

A mong its many components, worship includes an attentive and extended meditation on God's attributes, such as patience, love, holiness, and justice. We understand these characteristics because they have been described and demonstrated in God's Word and because we find them dimly echoed in ourselves.

The word *majesty* describes a reflected part of God's nature that emphasizes how different our Creator is from us. The Authorized Version uses the word twenty-seven times to convey words that can also be translated excellence, greatness, and honor. Majesty is not a quality of God that we observe primarily with our senses, but with our spirit. Majesty helps narrow our attention from worship as a general attitude to worship as a specific awareness of one overwhelming fact about God—His divine, royal position.

Even if we can't define majesty, the setting in the chorus allows us to grasp the meaning. Words like *glory, honor, praise, kingdom authority,* and *glorify* all point to Jesus' exalted position and role. The word *majesty* remains part of our worship vocabulary because we worship the King of kings. Even, and perhaps especially, among people who no longer use royalty as their social order, *majesty* helps describe one of those qualities of God we are not charged to imitate, but to deeply appreciate.

The LORD reigns, he is robed in majesty; the Lord is robed in majesty and is armed with strength. The world is firmly established; it cannot be moved.

PSALM 93:1

PRAYER

Alter the text of "Majesty" to personalize the song and turn it into a first-person expression of worship to Jesus. Experiment in prayer, using words related to royalty (like throne, crown, scepter, majesty, kingdom) to highlight and think about the unique and overwhelming privilege to know and be loved by the King of kings.

COME, NOW IS THE
TIME TO WORSHIP

Come, now is the time to worship.

Come, now is the time to give your heart.

Come, just as you are to worship.

Come, just as you are before your God.

Come.

—BRIAN DOERKSEN

This invitation is for each person. Amazing as it seems, Jesus calls us to come to Him just as we are. How accepting! How welcoming! How hard to do, sometimes!

In God's presence, we never have to be anything more than who we are. Satan works hard to convince us that we have to be more. Who hasn't, at some time, shunned God because of feeling unworthy? Thankfully, it's not our own merit on which we come. We come into God's presence by invitation. The blood of Jesus has stained the red carpet rolled out to us from God's throne. The One who paid for us to be cleansed invites us to come give our hearts to Him.

Satan will always tempt us to hide our true selves from God. He tells us to keep our doubts secret or hide our shame. He knows that once we realize that God accepts us as we are, his plans to keep us from God can't succeed.

As we tell God honestly how we feel, whether we're anxious about a difficulty, ashamed over our behavior, or doubtful of His love, he strips away our pretense and self-delusions. Then we can rejoice in our true identity—as God's beloved children.

You have no reason to hide. God invites you to come. Come—just as you are—to God.

Come, let us bow down in worship, let us kneel before the LORD our Maker.

PSALM 95:6

PRAYER

Thank God for inviting you to come to Him just as you are. And then come—in worship, in praise—giving your whole heart to Him.

H O L Y   G R O U N D

When I walked through the door,
I sensed His presence,
And I knew this was a place
Where love abounds.
For this is a temple,
Jehovah God abides here,
And we are standing in His presence
On holy ground.

—GERON DAVIS

When have you sensed God's presence? In a moment, alone in prayer? As you held a newborn baby? As you watched a stunning sunset? During that moment, you felt something that touched you deeply. Like Moses so long ago, you sensed that "the place where you are standing is holy ground" (Exodus 3:5).

How about when you walk through the door of your place of worship? Do you sense the presence of God? Do you feel that this is a place where love abounds, a temple where Jehovah God lives?

Of course, the Holy Spirit lives in every believer, so we are in God's presence no matter where we are. Yet as we gather to worship, our love for God and for others should overflow. Jesus taught, "Where two or three come together in my name, there am I with them" (Matthew 18:20).

To be in God's presence is to sense completeness, joy, and love. As we come into His presence to worship with fellow believers, let us come with a realization that we are on holy ground. May others who come discover that love abounds among believers, and may they want to join us!

You have made known to me the path of life; you will fill me with joy in your presence, with eternal pleasures at your right hand.

PSALM 16:11

PRAYER

Sit quietly and sense the Lord's presence. Pray that your church will become a place where God's presence is very real to all who enter there.

YOU ARE MY ALL IN ALL

You are my strength when I am weak,

You are the treasure that I seek,

You are my All in All.

Seeking You as a precious jewel,

Lord, to give up I'd be a fool,

You are my All in All.

—DENNIS JERNIGAN

We all need strength for our times of weakness. At times, when life overwhelms us, we feel that we can't go on. We need the One who can give us the strength to endure, to move ahead, to be victorious. Jesus can be our strength when we are weak.

Do you long for a love that never diminishes, regardless of how you act? What a treasure that would be! Would you like to live in a love so high and wide and deep and long that you never reach the end of it? Do you want to be so loved that you are pursued at any cost, even death? Many seek such love as though it were a precious jewel—a treasure beyond compare. This is the love Jesus offers.

Jesus can be our "All in All." He has enough strength for every difficulty. When we depend on Him we aren't disappointed. Tough times will come, and we may wonder how to get through another day. But, thankfully, we don't have to depend on ourselves or other people. With Jesus as our strength and our precious treasure, we can rest in knowing that He is always enough, today, tomorrow, and forever. He is our all in all.

The LORD is my strength and my shield; my heart trusts in him, and I am helped. My heart leaps for joy and I will give thanks to him in song.

PSALM 28:7

PRAYER

Ask God to remind you that He has all the strength you need. Thank Him for being your precious treasure.

WE WILL GLORIFY

We will glorify the King of kings,
We will glorify the Lamb.
We will glorify the Lord of lords,
Who is the great I AM.

Lord Jehovah reigns in majesty,
We will bow before His throne.
We will worship Him in righteousness,
We will worship Him alone.

—TWILA PARIS

Thomas Aquinas taught that God is pure act. In other words, whatever God is, God does. It is impossible for God's acts to be inconsistent with His character. For example, we may be patient people but have impatient moments. Not God. The great "I Am" is consistent, always the same. So we glorify our King, our Lord, the Lamb, worshiping Him alone because we can rely on Him 100 percent of the time.

No burden or need exists that His character can't meet. He doesn't have days off or suddenly decide to treat us differently. In fact, He is able to do much more than we could ever think or ask.

When we need a loving parent, He is our "Abba" Father (Romans 8:15).

When we're feeling insecure, He is a "sure foundation" (Isaiah 28:16).

When we're thirsty, He is our "spring" of living water (John 4:14).

When we're vulnerable, He is able to "keep [us] from falling" (Jude 24).

When we're lost, He is our "light" and our "salvation" (Psalm 27:1).

We get into trouble when we try to meet our needs ourselves! When we focus on God's amazing sufficiency, we find more than enough. He wants to fill us to overflowing. Thank God for being your great "I Am." He alone deserves your worship.

Every good and perfect gift is from above, coming down from the Father of the heavenly lights, who does not change like shifting shadows.

JAMES 1:17

PRAYER

As you review your needs, ask God to reveal an aspect of His character to you. Believe that He wants to be this for you today. Don't forget to praise Him for being so consistent.

G L O R I F Y   T H Y   N A M E

Father we love You,
We worship and adore You.
Glorify Thy name in all the earth.
Glorify Thy name, glorify Thy name,
Glorify Thy name in all the earth.

—DONNA ADKINS

No matter how hard we seek to glorify God in our everyday lives, our pride puts up a good fight. When someone forgets to acknowledge our effort, we often feel slighted. If we're asked to serve behind the scenes, we may squirm. We may even struggle with doing something just because God asked, and only doing that which brings us praise.

Thank God He knows how human we are! In His extreme grace, He uses us in spite of ourselves, even when our motives are less than pure.

As we ask Him to be glorified in our lives, little by little He changes our desires. Instead of caring about what we look like, we begin to care about protecting God's image. We honor His name and give Him full credit because we know that what people think of us isn't nearly as important as what they think about God. When He is glorified, lives are changed.

My soul will boast in the LORD; let the afflicted hear and rejoice. Glorify the LORD with me; let us exalt his name together.

PSALM 34:2, 3

PRAYER

Ask the Lord to make you willing to let go of your own glory and to glorify Him instead.

CHANGE MY HEART,
OH GOD

Change my heart, oh God;
Make it ever true.
Change my heart, oh God;
May I be like You.

You are the Potter,
I am the clay.
Mold me and make me,
This is what I pray.

—EDDIE ESPINOSA

Only the most courageous Christians sing this wholeheartedly. Like a potter working with clay, God will mold us if we yield to His touch. The touch of His hand transforms us, changing our hearts and making us more like Him. Sometimes God uses difficulties and trials in the shaping process. But all that we face is under the sovereign hand of the Potter.

When a difficulty strikes, we may wonder how to respond, what direction to turn. We may even devise a plan and take control. But God wants to use the situation to shape our hearts. God calls us to action, but He wants our hearts right first. When we focus on Him, we will do what is right.

As we yield to God's touch, we learn the lessons He wants to teach us: how to love those who may need it most, but deserve it least; how to believe the best of others instead of jumping to negative conclusions; how to see people's hurts instead of just the wounds they inflict.

This isn't easy! But as the Potter molds us, become more and more like Christ. And we find joy!

Yet, O LORD, you are our Father. We are the clay, you are the potter; we are all the work of your hand.

ISAIAH 64:8

PRAYER

Ask God to help you yield to His hand, molding and shaping your life. Ask Him to help you to see His sovereign hand in whatever you are facing today.

HE WHO BEGAN A GOOD WORK

If the struggle you're facing is slowly replacing
Your hope with despair,
Or the process is long and you're losing your song in
the night,
You can be sure
That the Lord has His hand on you, safe and secure,
He will never abandon you; you are His treasure
And He finds His pleasure in you.

He who began a good work in you,
He who began a good work in you
Will be faithful to complete it.
He'll be faithful to complete it.
He who started the work
Will be faithful to complete it in you.

—JON MOHR

Sometimes we have a song in the night. We can sing with joy and thankfulness. Our hearts are full. We feel God's blessings.

At other times, we lose that song. The night turns to a starless void. Our struggle, where we once held out hope, has caused us to despair. We have been patient, so patient, but the process has been so long that we just can't sing anymore. The weight is too heavy to carry.

Our difficulty may cause us to question God's love and protection. We feel as though we have been forgotten, lost somewhere in the darkness. But God never abandons us. We are like priceless pearls to Him—"his treasure."

God never forgets us, never gives up on us. Again and again he offers His fiery love to burn away impurities in our hearts and to draw us back to Himself. As we come to know and rely on God's love, we find our fears and doubts replaced with hope. Our struggles dim as we bask in His great love.

God never stops working, and He finds great pleasure in us. No matter how difficult the struggle seems today, remember that God has His hand on you—that means you are safe and secure, no matter how dark the night.

By day the LORD directs his love, at night his song is with me—a prayer to the God of my life.
                                    PSALM 42:8

PRAYER

Ask the Lord to give you a song in the night. Pray that you will sense His hand of safety and security, knowing that you are His greatest treasure.

SEEK YE FIRST

Seek ye first the kingdom of God
And His righteousness,
And all these things shall be added unto you.
Allelu, Alleluia.

Ask and it shall be given unto you,
Seek and ye shall find,
Knock and the door shall be opened unto
you.
Allelu, alleluia.

—KAREN LAFFERTY

Seek first the kingdom of God. In other words, make it a priority. It sure would feel safer if Jesus had said to take care of our needs first and then to look for ways to build His kingdom. That's because we want to give out of our overflow, after we know we have taken care of our needs. But Jesus tells us to put Him first, seeking His kingdom and His righteousness, trusting that He will meet our needs.

We can share honestly everything about ourselves with Christ, knowing that He will purify our hearts. His love is strong enough to mold our desires and to remove any obstacles that keep us from wanting His kingdom first.

So He invites us to *ask*—to tell Him all our desires, not just the spiritually correct ones. We may never know what Jesus thinks about them until we do. He invites us to *seek,* for only in the seeking can we find what we truly need. He invites us to *knock,* expecting Him to answer. We can only do that when we realize how much God loves us. He only has our best interests in mind. He isn't stingy, nor does He rejoice when He sees us in need. Like a loving father, He delights in caring for us, and He wants us to know He can be trusted.

But seek first his kingdom and his righteousness, and all these things will be given to you as well.

MATTHEW 6:33

PRAYER

Ask, seek, knock. Talk with the Lord about how you can seek first His kingdom and His righteousness, today and every day.

H O L Y   A N D
A N O I N T E D   O N E

Jesus, Jesus,

Holy and Anointed One, Jesus,

Jesus, Jesus,

Risen and Exalted One, Jesus.

Your name is like honey on my lips,

Your Spirit like water to my soul.

Your Word is a lamp unto my feet.

Jesus I love You, I love You.

—JOHN BARNETT

Wnat joy to sing the name of Jesus. His is a name above all names, a name so sweet it is like honey on our lips. The Bible promises that one day, "at the name of Jesus every knee should bow, in heaven and on earth and under the earth, and every tongue confess that Jesus Christ is Lord" (Philippians 2:10, 11).

To say His name should remind us of His great love for us—a love so great that He came from heaven to become like us in order to die for us. He sends His Holy Spirit into our thirsty souls to revive them and make them strong. He gives His Word, the Bible, to be a lamp to our feet, showing us just enough of the path ahead to step with confidence.

When the disciple Thomas believed after having seen and touched His risen Lord, Jesus said, "Blessed are those who have not seen and yet have believed" (John 20:29). We cannot see our Lord Jesus, and yet we believe in Him. Why? The sweetness of His name on our lips, the refreshment of the Spirit in our lives, the guidance of the Word on our steps.

Yes, Lord, we love you.

I will praise you, O Lord my God, with all my heart; I will glorify your name forever.

PSALM 86:12

PRAYER

Meditate on the sweetness of Jesus' name. Thank Him for the refreshment of his Holy Spirit. Praise Him for His Word that provides a lamp to your feet.

M O R E   P R E C I O U S
T H A N   S I L V E R

Lord, You are
More precious than silver.
Lord, You are
More costly than gold.
Lord, You are
More beautiful than diamonds,
And nothing I desire
Compares with You.

—LYNN DESHAZO

I magine being offered the world's greatest treasure, more precious than silver, more beautiful than diamonds. Imagine not having to do a thing to obtain this treasure because it had been bought by someone else. How thrilled would you be?

Actually, that has happened! God offers us the greatest treasure of all time: salvation. If you think salvation only means being guaranteed heaven and having your sins forgiven, you've barely scratched the surface of what is yours in Christ. Perhaps the greatest thrill of all is that Jesus gives us Himself.

The Life-giver, Dream-maker, Soul-changer, Wrong-righter comes to live in us. Out of Him flows a river of peace, an ocean of joy, a wellspring of hope. He promises to be our shepherd, our brother, our faithful friend, and our strong deliverer. Not only will He never fail us or forsake us, but He promises to call us, heal us, anoint us, bless us, cleanse us, prepare us, and fill us. He gives us His blood for holiness, His spirit for joy, and His mind for wisdom. The One who causes angels to fall prostrate before Him promises to reign over us, dwell in us, and walk beside us.

The more you go through with Jesus, the more valuable he becomes to you. What other treasure can compare with that?

Then the Almighty will be your gold, the choicest silver for you. Surely then you will find delight in the Almighty and will lift up your face to God.

JOB 22:25, 26

PRAYER

Tell Jesus He is your greatest treasure. Nothing you desire can compare with what you have already been given by Him.

A S   T H E   D E E R

As the deer panteth for the water,
So my soul longeth after Thee.
You alone are my heart's desire,
And I long to worship Thee.

You alone are my strength, my shield.
To you alone may my spirit yield.
You alone are my heart's desire,
And I long to worship Thee.

—MARTIN NYSTROM

Our fantasies deceive us. They tell us that if everything went our way, we would be satisfied. High pay, a glamorous house, and an exotic vacation all seduce us as worthwhile pursuits. In reality, even with all of that we would still feel empty. That's because quenching the soul's thirst with selfish pleasure is a lot like drinking salt water. The more we do it, the thirstier we become.

Jesus said, "Everyone who drinks this water will be thirsty again" (John 4:13). Only He can really quench our thirst. He knows that we are broken, thirsty, and needy, panting for refreshing water as a deer pants upon approaching a stream. So Jesus invites us to come and drink His love. When we worship Him, our cravings are met. By giving Him our praise and adoration, we find that our heart's desires are fulfilled.

Our worship need not end there. We can stay filled as we live each day by continually giving to God. Every time we yield to Him, we give Him more of ourselves and, in turn, experience more of His love. The world teaches that we feel fulfilled by giving in to ourselves. But only giving in to God brings soul-quenching satisfaction.

As the deer pants for streams of water, so my soul pants for you, O God.

PSALM 42:1

PRAYER

Ask Jesus to open your eyes when you begin to believe a lie about what will truly satisfy you. Thank Him for quenching your thirst.

C O M E   I N T O   H I S   P R E S E N C E

Come into His presence with thanksgiving in
your heart,
And give Him praise, and give Him praise.
Come into His presence with thanksgiving in
your heart,
Your voices raise, your voices raise.
Give glory and honor and power unto Him,
Jesus, the name above all names.

—L Y N N   B A I R D

O ften we treat thanksgiving as an extra in our time with God. We only praise Him if we have finished confessing our sins and laying out our requests and, then, have time left. As this song makes it clear, however, a thankful heart is the key to entering God's presence, the ticket to God's inner courts.

Everything God asks us to do is for our good and His glory. So when He tells us to praise Him, we can trust that He has our best interests in mind. As we reflect even on small events with a thankful heart, we're reminded that God is good, loving, faithful, and true. Soon our challenges will shrink in the light of who God is and what He has done for us. Sincere praise fans our small spark of faith into a blaze.

If we think of praise as a ticket, we will remember that we owe it to God. He is worthy of our constant admiration. If you can't see His hand at work in your situation, you can still praise Him for who He is and for what He will do in your life. God is always at work in you, drawing you to Himself. Even now, you only come because He initiated the relationship and because He gives you the strength to respond.

Thankful hearts aren't an option. As simple as this song seems, it's good advice!

I will praise God's name in song and glorify him with thanksgiving.

PSALM 69:30

PRAYER

Spend time in thankfulness and in praise for all that your Lord has done for you.

IN THE PRESENCE

In the presence of a holy God,
There's new meaning now to grace.
You took all my sins upon Yourself,
I can only stand amazed.

And I cry holy, holy, holy God,
How awesome is Your name.
Holy, holy, holy God,
How majestic is Your reign.
And I am changed,
In the presence of a holy God.

—MARK ALTROGGE

This powerful song teaches much about God. We get mere glimpses of God's holiness on this side of eternity, but we couldn't bear to see any more of it. Like Isaiah who had a vision of God's throne, our first response would be, "I am ruined!" (Isaiah 6:5).

Our God is completely holy. He is perfect in all His ways. God's holiness so reveals our utter sinfulness that we would shrink at His presence. Even the angels, who live in God's presence continually, covered their faces with their wings lest they be overwhelmed and overcome (Isaiah 6:2). But only when we understand God's holiness can we really appreciate His grace toward us. As unclean as we are, He still invites us into His presence. Why? Because Jesus took all our sins upon Himself.

God's grace allows us to look honestly at our sinfulness in the light of unconditional acceptance and forgiveness. We don't have to fear letting God shine into the dark corners of our hearts. He knows who we are, and He knows who we will become with His help. As we come into the presence of our holy God, He examines our hearts, reaches into our lives, and takes hold of our motives. Then His truth changes us. No wonder we stand amazed.

Each of the four living creatures had six wings and was covered with eyes all around, even under his wings. Day and night they never stop saying: "Holy, holy, holy is the Lord God Almighty, who was, and is, and is to come."

REVELATION 4:8

PRAYER

Open your heart completely to God's holiness. Show Him what is churning inside you and let Him do what He needs to with it. You can trust Him.

G O D   W I L L   M A K E   A   W A Y

God will make a way, where there seems to
be no way.
He works in ways we cannot see.
He will make a way for me.
He will be my guide,
hold me closely to His side,
With love and strength for each new day,
He will make a way. He will make a way.

—DON MOEN

Have you ever become lost? Ever reached a dead end and felt trapped? Ever been in a situation from which there seemed to be no way out?

We have plenty of ability to get ourselves into trouble—and if we don't do it ourselves, others do it for us. But God specializes in making the impossible possible, the hopeless hopeful, and the end merely a new beginning.

"God will make a way," says the song, "where there seems to be no way." He can help us discover a pathway that moments before had been hidden. When we ask Him to be our guide and to keep us close, we will find that He has a way for us to walk. The path is not always guaranteed to be easy—in fact, sometimes it is fraught with dangers, falling rocks, or steep inclines. But always there is a way, and always He walks beside us. No matter how difficult the path, He provides the strength we need to get where we need to go. He clears the path and then takes our hand to guide us.

Let God make your way today, through that impossible, hopeless, difficult, dead-end situation. The path is there—you just haven't seen it yet. Ask Him to show it to you. He will.

I guide you in the way of wisdom and lead you along straight paths.

PROVERBS 4:11

PRAYER

Tell God that you need Him to show you His way. Ask Him to guide you, make a way, and then walk with you wherever the path may lead.

JESUS, NAME ABOVE ALL NAMES

Jesus, name above all names,
Beautiful Savior, glorious Lord,
Emmanuel, God is with us,
Blessed Redeemer, living Word.

—NAIDA HERN

How fitting that the name "Emmanuel" means "God with us." Jesus embodied what God's plan had been all along: to be with us. From the beginning of time, this has been God's desire. Genesis 3:8 tells of God walking with Adam and Eve in the Garden of Eden. Then sin separated this first man and woman from Him. Later, He told Moses to instruct His people, the Israelites, to "make a sanctuary for me, and I will dwell among them" (Exodus 25:8).

God wasn't content to be with just some of His people, however. So He sent his Son, Jesus, as the ultimate sacrifice for sin; then He sent His Holy Spirit, "the Spirit of truth" to live with us and be in us (John 14:17).

In addition, John reveals God's ultimate plan finally completed: "And I heard a loud voice from the throne saying, 'Now the dwelling of God is with men, and he will live with them'" (Revelation 21:3). Nothing can or ever will stop God from being with us.

God wants to share our lives and be invited into our hearts. He wants to laugh at our jokes and hang out in our homes. He enjoys our kids and understands our weaknesses. When others leave or reject us, He will stay. When we're angry with Him, He won't turn away. We go through nothing alone.

God is with us in our doubts, in our confusion, and even in our darkness. This has always been His plan. How do you respond to this message of love?

The virgin will be with child and will give birth to a son, and they will call him Immanuel"—which means, "God with us."

MATTHEW 1:23

PRAYER

Thank God for His awesome plan to never leave you. Even though you could never deserve so great a love, it has been freely offered to you. Take time to sense "God with you" today.

I WORSHIP YOU, ALMIGHTY GOD

I worship You, almighty God,
There is none like You.
I worship You, O Prince of Peace,
That is what I want to do.
I give You praise,
For You are my righteousness.
I worship You, almighty God,
There is none like You.

—SONDRA CORBETT WOOD

This song expresses a desire to worship God and give Him praise. Is that what you truly long to do—or are other activities a higher priority? What drives or motivates you? Most people can't answer that question. Sure, they can probably explain a specific decision based on available money and time. Beneath such obvious reasons, however, lie motivations rarely acknowledged. Usually these hidden motives determine our actions. It could be the need to achieve, the desire to prove one's worth, the push of a guilty conscience, or the drive of an unhealthy appetite.

When we are driven by such motives, praise and worship don't even seem to fit anymore. In effect, we give in to little, lesser gods without even realizing it. Misguided motivations can easily lead us astray.

God longs to free us from that trap. He invites us to worship Him. Then, as we do, He pours His worth into us. As He brings our hidden motivations to light, we can choose to replace them with the desire to please only Him. And this frees us from our fears and from living self-protecting, self-promoting lives.

God sets us free to live the abundant life, free to worship Him.

Whom have I in heaven but you? . . . And earth has nothing I desire besides you.

PSALM 73:25

PRAYER

Ask God to examine why you do what you do. Be sure to listen to His answers. You'll be amazed at how well He knows you and how much He loves you.

I L O V E Y O U , L O R D

I love You, Lord, and I lift my voice
To worship You. Oh my soul, rejoice!
Take joy my King in what You hear.
May it be a sweet, sweet sound
In Your ear.

—LAURIE KLEIN

How often do you say to Jesus, "I love you"? Amazingly, He receives joy when your soul rejoices. Your words are a sweet sound in His ear.

Jesus invites you to be His close friend. Do you dare accept such an invitation? He knows your personality, gifts, and circumstances so intimately that your relationship with Him won't be like any before or since. It is unique to you and Him. Other people can tell you about their experiences with God, but you can be sure that yours will differ. What He asks you to do will be especially designed for you. He speaks in a language you understand. He knows your needs and the desires of your heart.

What does He require of you in return? Oh, just everything—your total commitment, total devotion, total willingness to be lost in His love. His love goes two ways! He'll share His life with you if you'll ask Him what's on His heart and gladly carry it as your own, be willing to let your heart be broken by what breaks His, and make His glory your priority.

Jesus delights in your worship, even as you delight in His presence. So lift your voice in praise!

We love because he first loved us.

1 JOHN 4:19

PRAYER

Tell the Lord that you want to receive all the love that He has to give you, and that you want to love Him in return. Worship and adore Him; let your soul rejoice.

O H   L O R D ,   Y O U ' R E   B E A U T I F U L

O Lord, You're beautiful,

Your face is all I seek,

For when Your eyes are on this child,

Your grace abounds to me.

—KEITH GREEN

What hope keeps you going when life gets rough? This song tells us that we can seek the Lord's face and there, in His eyes, find the grace to go on.

Simeon sought the Lord's face. We read about him in Luke 2:25, shortly after the birth of Jesus. Simeon had waited his whole life to see God's plan unfold. The Holy Spirit had promised Simeon that he would see the Messiah, and that promise had kept his hope alive. Imagine Simeon's joy when, after a lifetime of obedience and longing, he looked into the face of Jesus!

Like Simeon, we, too, will one day see Jesus. Revelation 22:4 promises that we "will see his face." What better hope to keep our spirits refreshed than knowing we will see God. This truth transforms the hard work of serving Him into the sweet anticipation of being with Him. The One who called us and equips us will one day welcome us home.

Yet even today, God promises that we can see His face. The psalmist wrote, "Let your face shine on your servant; save me in your unfailing love" (Psalm 31:16). When you seek God's face, you will find it—in prayer, in His Word, in the kind word of a friend. Look closely today. Ask God to reveal His face to you.

My heart says of you, "Seek his face!" Your face, LORD, I will seek.

PSALM 27:8

PRAYER

Ask the Lord to show you His face today. Be ready for Him to reveal Himself in unexpected ways.

WHEN I LOOK INTO YOUR HOLINESS

When I look into Your holiness,
When I gaze into Your loveliness,
When all things that surround,
Become shadows in the light of You,

I worship You, I worship You.
The reason I live is to worship You.
I worship You, I worship You.
The reason I live is to worship You.

—WAYNE AND CATHY PERRIN

D o you want the joy of a close relationship with the Lord? That's easy enough to answer. The real question is, are you willing to do your part to get there? This song holds a key.

As we focus our hearts and our minds on worshiping God, we soon realize that nothing else is more important. Jesus affirmed that the most important commandment is, "Love the Lord your God with all your heart and with all your soul and with all your mind and with all your strength" (Mark 12:30). Far from restricting us, loving the Lord this way meets our deepest needs. Deeper than our need for answers, deeper than our need for relief, and deeper than our need for a miracle is our need to love God. We were created to do that. It's easy to let difficulties consume us, taking our focus off our loving Father. Whenever we push worship to the side, however, we lose our way and feel empty. The more wrapped in ourselves we become, the less satisfied we are. In contrast, when we unwrap and turn our focus to God, we discover real life. When we look into His holiness and gaze into His loveliness, everything else dims in comparison.

It's hard work to quiet all our other wants and just want God. But when we do, our lives are changed, our minds are renewed, and our spirits are refreshed. When we worship God, we find that He fulfills every need and every desire.

Come, let us bow down in worship, let us kneel before the LORD our Maker.

PSALM 95:6

PRAYER

Ask God to let His light shine so brightly into your heart that everything else fades in comparison. Ask Him to teach you how to truly worship Him.

OPEN OUR EYES

Open our eyes, Lord;
We want to see Jesus,
To reach out and touch Him
And say that we love Him.

—BOB CULL

We would love to see Jesus—perhaps that is a longing in your heart. Just to see Him, to reach out and touch Him, to say that you love Him.

The people of Jesus' day got to walk and talk with Him. Many touched Him—jostling against Him in the crowd, perhaps giving a friendly hug, or tentatively hoping to be healed. Many were touched by Him—receiving from Him restored limbs, sight, and freedom from demonic oppression. Jesus was a real person. He got tired and slept in the back of a boat; He felt the heat of the sun and needed to sit by a well and get a drink; He enjoyed a good meal.

That's the point: Jesus walked here as one of us, as a live human being, a man. But He was also more than a man—He was God. The Bible tells us that Jesus returned to heaven and now sits at God's right hand. And you know what He does? He intercedes for us because He understands our weaknesses. He is intimately involved in our lives—He loves us, understands us, helps us.

Do you want to see Jesus, to reach out and touch Him? Go to His Word. Read His promises and claim them for your own. Do you want to tell Jesus you love Him? He's only a prayer away!

Therefore, since we have a great high priest who has gone through the heavens, Jesus the Son of God, let us hold firmly to the faith we profess. For we do not have a high priest who is unable to sympathize with our weaknesses, but we have one who has been tempted in every way, just as we are—yet was without sin. Let us then approach the throne of grace with confidence, so that we may receive mercy and find grace to help us in our time of need.

HEBREWS 4:14–16

PRAYER

Tell Jesus you love Him. Reach out and touch Him through the pages of His Word.

SPIRIT OF THE
LIVING GOD

Spirit of the living God,

Fall afresh on me.

Spirit of the living God,

Fall afresh on me.

Melt me, mold me,

Fill me, use me.

Spirit of the living God,

Fall afresh on me.

—DANIEL IVERSON

I magine being one of Jesus' disciples when He breathed on them and gave them the Holy Spirit (John 20:22). With Jesus' breath, the disciples received the power and authority to bring His life to the world. Christ has also given us that authority. Because "all Scripture is God-breathed" (2 Timothy 3:16), we encounter the living Word every time we open the Bible. And God's Spirit breathes into us as we receive His truth.

This truth, the truth about Jesus, is meant to set us free (John 8:32)! We become all God wants us to be as we let the Holy Spirit apply His Word to our lives. We break out of old patterns and ways of thinking and are given newness and freshness. The Holy Spirit knows how to use Scripture to melt us, mold us, and set us free.

Instead of being fearful about what God may do in us, we can be assured that He wants to bring us into new levels of freedom. He wants to melt our resistance to change, mold our desires to higher purposes, fill us with the power to live an abundant life, and use us beyond what we could imagine. All that, and heaven, too!

Look into God's Word and heed Jesus' words from John 20: "Receive the Holy Spirit."

Now the Lord is the Spirit, and where the Spirit of the Lord is, there is freedom.

2 CORINTHIANS 3:17

PRAYER

Ask God to remove any fear you might have of letting Him change you. Pray that His Holy Spirit will fall fresh on you, today and every day, bringing fresh newness to life.

WE WORSHIP AND ADORE THEE

We worship and adore Thee,

Bowing down before Thee,

Songs of praises singing,

Alleluias ringing.

Alleluia, alleluia, alleluia,

Amen.

—AUTHOR UNKNOWN

In order to truly worship and adore our God, in order to bow down before Him, we need complete humility. We need to acknowledge that we don't know it all or have it all. We need to recognize that He is in authority, and we need to be willing to obey.

"Obedience" and "authority" don't sound positive or enjoyable. Being rebellious and self-centered by nature, we want what we want when we want it. And what we want most is control. We don't naturally give in to letting God decide what's best for us. It seems that our way has to fail before we finally understand and then follow God's way. Only then do we realize that not only are we not in charge, but we're just a small part of a much bigger picture.

God should be our ultimate authority. Only He sees the end from the beginning. Only He has a good plan for our lives. Only He has the power to bring it about. When we bow before God, we submit ourselves to His control.

As difficult as it is to give up control, doing so brings great relief. Now we can give up trying to run our world. In addition, we don't have to know all the answers and aren't responsible for changing other people. We only need to trust and obey. Such simplicity makes life sweet!

Take your rightful place at God's feet and let your heart fill with praise.

All the ends of the earth will remember and turn to the LORD, and all the families of the nations will bow down before him.

PSALM 22:27

PRAYER

Acknowledge God alone as your authority. Worship Him, thank Him, praise Him, and obey Him.

YES WE ALL AGREE

Oh Lord, we agree,
In the power and strength of unity
That You're worthy, worthy of our praise.
Oh Lord, we agree,
With our whole hearts we proclaim to Thee
That you are the King, the only Lord,
The only God who's holy.
We agree that
You're worthy of all our praise.

—TOMMY WALKER

For what clues do you look to determine whether the people you meet are believers? Key words? A church name? Christian jewelry?

The apostle John had much clearer criteria. John knew that all the peripheral issues aren't nearly as important as this: What do people think about Jesus? "If anyone acknowledges that Jesus is the Son of God, God lives in him and he in God" (1 John 4:15). When we know that someone acknowledges that Jesus is the Son of God, that is the only issue that really matters. Opinions may differ on a whole range of other issues, but Christians who agree on Jesus can sing with one voice "in the power and strength of unity."

Unity is powerful. Unified, the church can prevail; torn by division, it will fall (Luke 11:17). No wonder Jesus prayed so sincerely for His followers to be one. When we let our differences divide us, we forget who our real enemy is and start attacking each other.

How silly, when no one is perfect and perfectly correct. Praise God, we don't depend on that! The gospel is not about who is better or more correct, but about grace and about Jesus. God works for us and in us despite our faults and shortcomings, and, in His great mercy, He continues to work through us. Let us rejoice in our Savior, humbly joining with others who affirm Christ as Savior, with our whole hearts proclaiming Him worthy of our praise.

I pray also for those who will believe in me through their message, that all of them may be one, Father, just as you are in me and I am in you. I have given them the glory that you gave me, that they may be one as we are one.

JOHN 17:20b-22

PRAYER

Ask God to see your oneness in Christ with other believers.

J E S U S ,   L O V E R
O F   M Y   S O U L

Jesus, Lover of my soul,

I love You, I need You.

Jesus, I will never let You go

Though my world may fall.

You've taken me from the miry clay,

I'll never let You go.

You've set my feet upon the rock,

My Savior, my closest friend,

And now I know I will worship You

until the very end.

—JOHN EZZY, DANIEL GRUL, AND STEPHEN MCPHERSON

What God did before, He still does today. Those who have had God pull them out of the "miry clay" know how much they need Him. It is a defining experience. Up to that point, they may have squeaked by knowing all the right answers or having a godly heritage. But when all of one's good efforts prove useless, real faith begins. Everything before this experience was self-reliance; after all, it's all God-reliance.

God saves us when we are at our weakest so that we'll learn to rely on His love. We see that He is stronger than our sin and more real than our circumstances. Personal abilities, favorable circumstances, worldly success, and people's love, will all let us down. If we depend on them, we'll be up when they're strong and down when they're weak.

Only total reliance on our soul's lover can give us true stability. Once we have that, we have a source of strength that will endure. Trusting in God's unchanging love gives us the security we need. If your feet are planted on Him, your Rock, you can say with glad determination, "Come what may, I'll never let You go."

I will declare that your love stands firm forever, that you established your faithfulness in heaven itself.

PSALM 89:2

PRAYER

Do you feel mired in life? Ask God to help you remember the words of God to Paul: "My grace is sufficient for you, for my power is made perfect in weakness." Ask Him to give you a heart that responds, "Therefore I will boast all the more gladly about my weaknesses, so that Christ's power may rest on me" (2 Corinthians 12:9b).

T H E R E   I S   N O N E   L I K E   Y O U

There is none like You.
No one else can touch
My heart like You do.
I could search for all eternity long,
And find there is none like You.

—Lenny LeBlanc

These words describe someone totally in love with Jesus. Do you sense the songwriter's longing to be with the one he loves? Such a close relationship doesn't happen quickly. It's nurtured through careful, deliberate time together.

How much time do you devote to listening to God? Do you feast on His Word? Not just quickly skimming the verses but lingering and savoring them? Are you letting Scripture check your thoughts and attitudes? Have you allowed it to transform your priorities? Is God's Word your guide in determining decisions? Hopefully you are able to say with Moses, "They are not just idle words for you—they are your life" (Deuteronomy 32:47a).

The measure you use will be measured back to you. If you want Jesus to be your everything, then make Him more important than anything. When we give Him prime time (not leftover time), speak from the heart, and listen carefully for His answers, He will meet us and touch us.

Daily, the riches of His glory await you. His Word can take you deeper and higher than you've ever been. Your time together will become the best part of every day. There is no one like Him.

Among the gods there is none like you, O Lord; no deeds can compare with yours.

PSALM 86:8

PRAYER

Ask God to develop your relationship with Him as you spend time in the Bible. Ask Him, "Is there something you want to teach me about this?" Wait and listen for His answer.

I WILL PRAISE YOUR NAME

I will magnify, I will glorify,
I will lift on high
Your name, Lord Jesus.

For Your love is never ending
And Your mercy ever true.
I will bless Your name, Lord Jesus,
For my heart belongs to You.

—BOB FITTS

Without a doubt, the most powerful word in the world is "Jesus." By calling on His name, we are saved (Romans 10:13). Trusting in it frees us from the strangleholds of legalism, shame, and pride. When we embrace it, we overcome our self-centeredness. No other name rules like Jesus.

The book of Acts records mighty deeds done in Jesus' name: casting out demons, healing the sick, and conquering sin. The power of Jesus' name threatened the authorities so much that they tortured, beat, and jailed the disciples in attempts to get them to stop using it.

Eventually, at the name of Jesus, Satan will be utterly defeated. Every knee in heaven and on earth and under the earth will bow and every tongue will confess that Jesus is Lord (Philippians 2:10), all because of the name, "Jesus."

This truth is so simple and yet so profound. No matter what comes against us, we have Jesus. No matter how hard the road or how dark the night, we have Jesus. He can't be put off by our sin or doused by our doubt. He won't be thwarted by injustice or defeated by Satan. He is eternal, unchanging, inexorable, and victorious.

Jesus! Praise His name. Come into agreement with all that He is. This is the heart of worship—not fancy music or lengthy prayers, but the name of God's precious Son on your lips. Lift Him up and bless His name.

Therefore I will praise you among the nations, O LORD; I will sing praises to your name.
PSALM 18:49

PRAYER

Tell Jesus that you want to know all the riches of His name: its power to delight, release, forgive, heal, and overcome. Ask Him to teach you to honor and revere His name above all else.

IN MOMENTS LIKE THESE

In moments like these,

I sing out a song,

I sing out a love song to Jesus.

In moments like these,

I lift up my hands,

I lift up my hands to the Lord.

Singing, "I love You, Lord."

—DAVID GRAHAM

When is the best time to tell Jesus that we love Him? It may be in moments when we contemplate His great love for us. At these times, it's as if the screen between now and eternity is lifted and we get a glimpse of how Christ treasures us.

Think of Christ's love for you and sense His pleasure. Feel His desire to share His dreams with you and how He can't wait to show you heaven. Know that He wants to bless you and that He wishes you would hold still long enough for Him to give you all He desires. Imagine Him looking at your life and swelling with pride at all He's done. These are great moments to tell Jesus, "I love you, Lord!"

In contrast, our struggles present another great time to express our love for Christ. Everyone has unpleasant relationship issues, frustrating circumstances, and painful tragedies. That's when we should make a conscious choice to express our love for Jesus. Lifting our hands, like little children, we can say, "I love you, Lord." We experience freedom when we love Him even when life seems upside-down.

Sometimes Jesus has you by the hand and you can sense His smile. Other times He has you in His arms, carrying you through difficulties. In moments like these, or anytime in between, tell Jesus you love Him. He is always with you. Sing out a song of love to your Lord.

I love you, O LORD, my strength.

PSALM 18:1

PRAYER

Let God examine your love for Him. He can show you why you have held back and help you overcome. The more you love the Lord, the easier it becomes. And the easier it becomes, the more you will love Him.

SURELY THE PRESENCE
OF THE LORD

Surely the presence
Of the Lord is in this place.
I can feel His mighty power
And His grace.
I can hear the brush of angels' wings;
I see glory on each face.
Surely the presence
Of the Lord is in this place.

—LANNY WOLFE

The overwhelming awareness of God's "mighty power" . . . the light "brush of angels' wings"—sensing God's presence brings unexplainable peace and joy.

Those who know God recognize His presence the best. We can quickly recognize the presence of our loved ones. They are close to us, crossing paths with us every day. We know the sound of the voice; we recognize the handwriting. We can pick out the laugh in a crowd or even the scent of perfume or aftershave.

God's personality has many subtleties as well. The more familiar you become with Him, especially His work in your life, the easier you will find it to recognize His work in others. Because He has pardoned your guilt, you will identify the look of someone at peace with God. Because He has restored your dignity, you will be able to see His glory in others. If He has delivered you from an abusive past, you know how a hardened face can be transformed by joy.

Do you want to sense more of God's presence in your life? Get to know Him better. You'll soon see the evidence of His power and grace everywhere you turn.

Blessed are those who have learned to acclaim you, who walk in the light of your presence, O Lord.

PSALM 89:15

PRAYER

Thank Jesus for giving you the ability to recognize His voice, and confess anything that may be blocking your ability to hear Him.

HERE IN YOUR PRESENCE

Here in Your presence,

Beholding Your glory,

Bowing in reverence,

We worship You only.

Standing before You,

We love and adore You, O Lord,

There is none like You.

—DON MOEN

When we bow before God, everything is put into perspective. Certainly the way is not easy—something always threatens to put our lives on tilt. So we scramble to get back our balance, thinking if we could just get this one thing right, we'd be okay. If we let ourselves focus for too long on the frustrations, problems, fears, and worries, we soon would feel overwhelmed and anxious.

But we have a refuge, the Lord Himself. Focusing on God and His love for us brings us relief and peace. We stand in awe and wonder of who He is.

No one is like the Lord. As we respond to His great love—laughing with Him, crying out to Him, humbling ourselves before Him, being awed by Him—we realize that His presence changes everything. Worship awakens us to new truths and helps put our troubles in perspective. But most of all, we find joy in spending time with God. Nothing and no one is more exciting or more wonderful. No relationship is more intimate or faithful.

Don't wait for life to be perfect, for everything to fall into place. Find your peace and joy in God's presence.

You will show me the path of life; in Your presence is fullness of joy; at Your right hand are pleasures forevermore.

PSALM 16:11 (NKJV)

PRAYER

Thank God for the power of His presence. Enjoy being with Him. Stand before Him, loving and adoring Him.

F A T H E R ,   I   A D O R E   Y O U

Father, I adore You,
Lay my life before You.
How I love You.

Jesus, I adore You,
Lay my life before You.
How I love You.

Spirit, I adore You,
Lay my life before You.
How I love You.

—TERRYE COELHO STROM

How often do you truly lay your life before Jesus? Is your life an open book, revealing everything about you? Even if you choose not to do so—hoping to hide something back—Jesus already knows. He knows your sins; He knows you need His forgiveness; He knows your heart and your desires. Once you understand the breadth of Christ's knowledge and the depth of His love, you will love Him even more.

It's human nature to try and justify our questionable motives and to attribute our sins to mere quirkiness. But the Holy Spirit breaks our pride as He convicts us. We gain humility as we catch a glimpse of God's grace and forgiveness. Instead of rejecting us, He works with us. Instead of condemning our actions, He looks at our thoughts and motives and shows us what needs to change. How can we help but love a just, perfect, and holy God who binds Himself to sinners like us?

Instead of being afraid to let God find out what's wrong inside, we can lay our lives before Him with confidence. Then He will reveal even more reasons to love Him.

If we confess our sins, he is faithful and just and will forgive us our sins and purify us from all unrighteousness.

1 JOHN 1:9

PRAYER

Spend a few minutes adoring our loving heavenly Father and laying your life before Him.

I Stand in Awe

You are beautiful beyond description,
too marvelous for words,
Too wonderful for comprehension,
like nothing ever seen or heard.
Who can grasp Your infinite wisdom?
Who can fathom the depth of Your love?
You are beautiful beyond description,
majesty enthroned above.

And I stand, I stand in awe of You,
I stand, I stand in awe of You.
Holy God, to whom all praise is due,
I stand in awe of You.

—Mark Altrogge

o questions like these percolate in the back of your mind: "What will I do if I lose my job?" "What can I look forward to this week?" "Can I afford to buy what I want?"

We desire security. We enjoy recreation. We want to possess beauty. God designed us to experience all this. It's part of our innate desire to live life to the fullest.

Unless we're careful, however, the drives meant to push us toward God can lead us into pursuing the world's counterfeits. The world tells us to put our reliance in a steady paycheck or plan the perfect event or buy another item we don't need. Even though we know these can't satisfy us, we fall for that line again and again.

Only God can live up to all our hopes. The more we enjoy Him, the freer we are to enjoy life's other pleasures for what they are— extras, not necessary for our satisfaction. Then, when the job falls through, the plans get cancelled, or the new gismo becomes outdated, we can still have joy. We don't need perfection from anything else when the Perfect One is satisfying us.

The next time you grasp for security, focus on God's majesty and awesomeness. When you long for good or goods, remind yourself of your wonderful Lord. And when you yearn for beauty, fix your eyes on the One who is beautiful beyond description. Stand in awe of Him. Let Him meet your deepest desires.

Dominion and awe belong to God; he establishes order in the heights of heaven.

JOB 25:2

PRAYER

Stand in awe of God. Meditate on His beauty, wisdom, and love. Then praise Him.

COME LET US ADORE HIM /
THOU ART WORTHY

O come, let us adore Him,
O come, let us adore Him,
O come, let us adore Him,
Christ the Lord.

For He alone is worthy,
For He alone is worthy,
For He alone is worthy,
Christ the Lord.

Thou art worthy,
Thou art worthy,
Thou art worthy, O Lord,
To receive glory,
Glory and honor,
Glory and honor and power.

—PAULINE MILLS

Singing, "O come let us adore Him," we usually think of Christmas. And we picture the Magi bowing to Jesus, laying their treasures of gold, frankincense, and myrrh before Him. We would never picture them stopping half-way to Bethlehem saying, "I'm too tired," "This is taking way too long," or "I have better things I could be doing."

We smile at how lame that would sound. If we were really honest, however, we would have to admit that we let similar excuses stop us from true worship. But all our excuses fade in light of the one reason to worship Him: He is worthy!

As we honor God, we discover a great mystery of the Christian life: If we're willing to overcome the obstacles to worship (whether schedule or problems), God will take care of the things that had kept us from it. Will these statements be true for you? "I'm going to enjoy God whether or not I have all the answers to my problems." "I'm going to put Him first whether or not it means I get my stuff done today." "I'm going to take the next step whether or not I know where it will lead." That's living by faith! Come and adore Him!

You are worthy, our Lord and God, to receive glory and honor and power.

REVELATION 4:11a

PRAYER

Spend time simply adoring Christ, your Lord.

OH THE GLORY OF YOUR PRESENCE

Oh the glory of Your presence,

We Your temple, give You rev'rence.

Come and rise from Your rest,

And be blessed by our praise.

As we glory in Your embrace,

As Your presence now fills this place.

—STEVE FRY

The Israelites had a day they would never forget. When the Ark of the Covenant was brought into Solomon's newly built temple, "the priests could not perform their service because of the cloud, for the glory of the LORD filled his temple" (1 Kings 8:11). They were so overwhelmed with God's presence that it knocked them off their feet!

As believers, we are God's temple, and He fills us with His glory through the Holy Spirit. Paul explained it this way: "Do you not know that your body is a temple of the Holy Spirit, who is in you, whom you have received from God? You are not your own; you were bought at a price. Therefore honor God with your body" (1 Corinthians 6:19, 20).

We experience the glory of God's presence in our lives when we live His way. So, before rushing in and asking Him to bless us again, we may need to ask ourselves some tough questions: "Am I involved with something (or someone) God wouldn't approve?" "Am I not doing something I should be doing?" "Is God pleased with the way I am acting?"

With obedience there is no automatic pilot. It will take a constant dialogue between you and God to know what He wants and to carry it out. Then, as you live according to God's will, you'll experience life's greatest reward: the glory of His presence.

And in him you too are being built together to become a dwelling in which God lives by his Spirit.

EPHESIANS 2:22

PRAYER

Ask God to examine your actions, your thoughts, and your motives. Tell Him that as His holy temple, you want to live to glorify Him.

WE BOW DOWN

We bow down and we crown You the King,
We bow down and we crown You the King,
We bow down and we crown You the King,
King of all kings You will be!

—TWILA PARIS

What kind of a king would insist on making you an heir to all he owns? What kind of a king invites his subjects not only into his palace but also into intimate fellowship with himself? What kind of a king would see everything his people lack and constantly say, "Here, take mine." What kind of a king says, "I'm here for you. Just call."

Only the King of kings! The one who keeps His subjects by His extreme kindness, overflowing tenderness, and unlimited compassion.

Why would we ever refuse to bow to such a king? So we could go back to striving to achieve our worth? So we could depend on ourselves and claw our way to the top? So we could relive the envy and anger we harbored against others? Oh, aren't you glad that you're saved! Aren't you relieved that instead of harsh pursuits, you know the joy of being blessed? Jonah 2:8 says it best: "Those who cling to worthless idols forfeit the grace that could be theirs."

Our God is a gracious King. You can stop striving and let Him give you what you need. You can come to Him and find rest from all your futile efforts. Grace is His to give. The King will do for you what you could never do for yourself. He will heal, bless, restore, and cleanse. What more could you want but to bow down and thank Him for being your King?

For he has rescued us from the dominion of darkness and brought us into the kingdom of the Son he loves.

COLOSSIANS 1:13

PRAYER

As you bow before Jesus, ask Him for what you need. His resources of strength, joy, and peace are endless. Believe that He wants to share them with you.

BE EXALTED, O GOD

I will give thanks to Thee,
O Lord, among the people.
I will sing praises to Thee among the
nations.
For Thy steadfast love is great,
It is great to the heavens,
And Thy faithfulness,
Thy faithfulness to the clouds.

—BRENT CHAMBERS

If you have ever been with someone who has recently fallen in love, you know that every other word out of the person's mouth seems to be about the new relationship. With starry-eyed enthusiasm, the person describes every detail, sometimes again and again!

That's a wonderful picture of how passionate God wants us to be about Him. All through Scripture, people just couldn't keep quiet about their love for God. David wrote psalms while his enemies were pursuing him. Paul encouraged the churches while he was imprisoned. Others were tortured and exiled, but they all focused on their love for the Lord. What could explain their commitment? Only a powerful love that had swept them away.

Every believer has a story to tell. What has God brought you through? How has He shown you His love? What unshakeable quality of His nature do you rely on? Ponder these facts. Be thankful for them. Let them sink into your heart and delight you. Then, maybe the next time you feel like singing praises to God in public, or bringing up the "G" word in conversation, you won't stop. You'll be so in love with God that the world hears it—again and again. What better testimony could there be?

Your love, O LORD, reaches to the heavens, your faithfulness to the skies.

PSALM 36:5

PRAYER

Ask God to open your eyes to His love that always surrounds you. As you go through your day, acknowledge every reminder that He cares for you. Thank Him and tell Him you love Him, too.

BLESSED BE THE NAME
OF THE LORD

Blessed be the name of the Lord,

He is worthy to be praised and adored.

So we lift up holy hands in one accord,

Singing, "Blessed be the name, blessed be the name,

Blessed be the name of the Lord."

—DON MOEN

Worship is contagious. It just takes one person, willing to be vulnerable to God and the people around, to infect a whole group.

Throughout Scripture, the people who led worship had to take some risks. Moses broke out in song after crossing the Red Sea—a bold move for a reluctant leader with a stutter. David, overcome with joy, danced before the Lord, not caring whether or not it made him look foolish. Daniel openly worshiped God even though it meant putting his life on the line.

For each of these men, fears of what they might look like or how they might be labeled or what might become of them could not hold them back. As a result, whole nations were led into God's presence. Lives were saved, and people were directed back to God.

Have you ever stopped to consider the effect your worship might have on those around you? Your praise can help lift their spirit of heaviness or give them the hope they need for their future. You might make the difference between their pressing on or giving up.

God is looking for true worshipers who will bless His name. Will you be the one to shout out loud and not hold back? Could this be your song?

Blessed be the name of the LORD from this time forth and for evermore.

PSALM 113:2 (KJV)

PRAYER

What risks are you willing to take to worship God? Let God examine what might hold you back and ask Him to help make your worship pleasing to Him alone.

HE IS LORD

He is Lord, He is Lord,
He is risen from the dead,
And He is Lord.
Every knee shall bow, every tongue confess,
That Jesus Christ is Lord.

—TRADITIONAL

ometimes we can feel like walking away from God. Sorrows threaten to break us. Grief sneaks up on us. Unfair treatment takes us by surprise. We want to protest, "This wasn't supposed to be so difficult!"

Jesus never promised that it would be easy. In fact, the first disciples soon discovered that following Him turned out to be tougher than anyone had expected. When disappointments overwhelm us, we may feel like we want a new god. But the fact remains that He is Lord whether we like it or not. Our only choices are to be angry and alienate our only source of help or to bow to the mystery and follow Him as Lord.

By following Him through the tough times, you will discover this wonderful truth: Life may feel like a roller coaster, but the people who trust the safety belts enjoy the ride. Even through steep dives and dark tunnels, you need not fear. He is Lord over the things that threaten to destroy you, and He is Lord over anything that could separate you from His love.

Jesus didn't come to make our lives more difficult. He came to give us the security we need to live them with joy. You can abandon yourself to His plans, knowing that Jesus Christ is Lord.

They will make war against the Lamb, but the Lamb will overcome them because he is Lord of lords and King of kings—and with him will be his called, chosen and faithful followers.

REVELATION 17:14

PRAYER

Is life difficult today? Confess your frustration and ask Jesus to take over and be Lord of your life. Then trust Him, and begin to enjoy the ride.

IN HIS TIME

In His time, in His time,
He makes all things beautiful
In His time.
Lord, please show me every day,
As You're teaching me Your way,
That You do just what You say,
In Your time.

—DIANE BALL

What parent hasn't been asked by an anxious child in the back seat, "When will we be there?" We understand our children's desire to arrive. Maybe that's why we, as God's children, ask Him, "When will this be over?" We want so badly to just get through the difficult times and reach the final destination.

God has His own timetable. His plan is established, and He's eager for us to get with it. Living in step with the Holy Spirit, we work in sync with Him. Every time we lay down our sense of timing and willingly take up God's, we move into a plan much greater than ourselves. Doors open. Needs are met. Even small details fall into place.

But this requires that we give up our desire to hurry events. God's plan isn't to rush us through our troubles. It's to take those troubles and use them to make something beautiful for us. Don't give up just short of God's time! It may be just a little while until you see God turn your anger into peace, your weariness into rest, your dread into hope, your loneliness into belonging, and your disgrace into honor. The Christian life isn't just about sorrow and suffering, but about God's ability to make all things beautiful in His time.

Will you give God the time to do that?

God has made everything beautiful for its own time. He has planted eternity in the human heart, but even so, people cannot see the whole scope of God's work from beginning to end.
ECCLESIASTES 3:11 (NLT)

PRAYER

While God may never answer our questions of "when?" and "why?" He will answer, "What do you want me to learn from this?" If you're going through a difficult time, ask Him that today. Then listen for the beauty He wants to bring in your life—in His time.

I W I L L   C O M E   A N D
B O W   D O W N

I will come and bow down at Your feet,

Lord Jesus.

In Your presence is fullness of joy.

There is nothing, there is no one who

compares to You.

I take pleasure in worshiping You, Lord.

—M A R T I N   J.   N Y S T R O M

I n Jesus' presence, we find joy. Not condemnation, not guilt, not fear—but *joy!* Think about it. Jesus wants us to enjoy our relationship with Him. He wants us to delight in Him as He delights in us. He plans for us to inherit every possible spiritual blessing!

Feeling blessed doesn't sit well with joyless friends. They are much more comfortable when we feel badly about our sinfulness. They live under condemnation, so they want our company in their misery. But they're missing out on the joy! In God's presence, we find that the price has been paid in full! Nothing is left for us to do but to confess our sin and then let it go, moving on to enjoying life in Christ.

When we bow before Jesus, we find that He more than makes up for all that we lack. We can face our unworthiness because we know the Grace-Giver. We can acknowledge our brokenness because we know the Healer. We can deal with all that our sin has ruined because we know the One who makes all things new. All that we need is in Him.

So throw wide open the door to your heart and dance with Him, sing to Him, and rejoice in how He fills you. In His presence, find fullness of joy!

Surely you have granted him eternal blessings and made him glad with the joy of your presence.
PSALM 21:6

PRAYER

Jesus invites you to rejoice when you are weak because He is still strong, to rejoice when you're defeated because He is still victorious, and to rejoice when you feel lost because He still knows the way. Find the freedom, the relief, and the pleasure of worshiping at His feet.

C O M E   L E T   U S   W O R S H I P
A N D   B O W   D O W N

Come, let us worship and bow down,
Let us kneel before the Lord our God, our
Maker.
For He is our God and we are the people of
His pasture,
And the sheep of His hand, just the sheep of
His hand.

—DAVE DOHERTY

Sheep depend on their shepherd. He leads them to food and shelter and protects them from enemy attacks. If it weren't for the shepherd's care, sheep would be hopeless and helpless. Maybe that's why the Bible so often refers to God's people as His sheep. We simply weren't designed to be self-sufficient.

Our Good Shepherd knows this. He doesn't expect us to live or even survive on our own. On the contrary, He expects us to ask for help. Our neediness never surprises Him, and our asking does not put Him off. But when sheep think they know better than the shepherd, they get into trouble. They wander off and get lost, or worse, become captured by a lion or a wolf. They fall into ravines; they drown in streams. When we think we know better than God, we experience the consequences.

Did you know your needs are God's problem? The Good Shepherd is waiting to help you. He will come to your aid. No request is too large or too small.

People who remember that they're just sheep make their requests; then they lie down in a green pasture and rest. That's the life God wants us to have. He wants to be our Good Shepherd. Find the comfort of being His precious lamb.

For he is our God; and we are the people of his pasture, and the sheep of his hand.

PSALM 95:7 (KJV)

PRAYER

What do you need today? Better treatment? Financial support? Improved health? Tell your Good Shepherd about it. Acknowledge that because you are one of His sheep, it's His problem, and ask Him to do something about it.

ONLY BY GRACE

Into Your presence You call us,
Into Your presence You draw us.
And now by Your grace we come,
Now by Your grace we come.

—GERRIT GUSTAFSON

You have been summoned into God's presence. He has called you and drawn you, and you have come. God has put a longing in your heart to know Him better, and by His grace He allows you to come.

Grace is God's favor, offered as a gift. We cannot earn it or buy it. We could never deserve it no matter how hard we might try. We can only accept this gift freely and gratefully.

God pours out His grace so consistently that we sometimes take it for granted. By grace He overlooks our faults, extends undeserved kindness, and opens the door into His presence. Far from an automatic response, God chooses to be gracious to us countless times each day. What an enormous favor that is!

Our obedience goes up and down. We get on track and off. Yet God's grace never wavers. Grace is never reluctant, never absent, even for a moment. If it were, we would be utterly destroyed. Thankfully, God's treatment of us has nothing to do with who we are and everything to do with who He is: consistently good, unfailingly merciful, abounding in grace—grace that is always loving, always present, always faithful.

Come into His presence—you have been summoned there by your God of all grace.

For it is by grace you have been saved, through faith—and this not from yourselves, it is the gift of God.

EPHESIANS 2:8

PRAYER

Come into God's presence. Ask God to remind you of His abundant grace toward you. Thank Him for all He has done for you—all because of His grace.

YOU ARE MY
HIDING PLACE

You are my hiding place;
You always fill my heart
With songs of deliverance.
Whenever I am afraid,
I will trust in You.

—MICHAEL LEDNER

When life gets to be too much, when you are afraid, do you need a refuge? God can be your hiding place. When you are with Him, He fills your heart with joyful songs, replacing your fear with trust and peace.

Satan would like you to be afraid. He would like you to think that seeking a hiding place in God is cowardly. He wants you paralyzed by fear and afraid to turn to God for help. And he wants you to be ashamed of your fear.

But it's all right to feel afraid. God knows that having sweaty palms and racing hearts are part of being human and how He created us. God asks us to bring our fears to Him and to hide in Him.

In God's presence we find the strength to confront our fears. When we run to Him, He reveals the truth behind what frightens us. In the light of knowing His goodness and trusting His love, fears are revealed for what they are: mere balloons, inflated to appear much larger than reality. As God points out His truth, He pops each one.

What fears hold you back? God can get you through any difficulty if you'll trust in Him. Run to your hiding place. Trust in His truth.

You are my hiding place; you will protect me from trouble and surround me with songs of deliverance.
PSALM 32:7

PRAYER

The psalm writer often wrote of what he would do. "I will trust in you" (Psalm 56:3). "I will sing to the LORD" (Psalm 13:6). "I will sing praises to your name" (Psalm 18:49). Ask God to show you what to do the next time you feel afraid. Ask Him to be your hiding place and to show you His truth.

I S N ' T   H E ?

Isn't He beautiful,
Beautiful, oh isn't He?
Prince of Peace, Son of God,
Isn't He?
Isn't He wonderful,
Wonderful, oh isn't He?
Counselor, Almighty God,
Isn't He, isn't He?

—JOHN WIMBER

How can we be friends with this infinitely holy, always perfect God? Even on good days, we probably make someone angry. Without even trying, we disappoint people. Between the cracks of our intentional living, careless words slip out.

Then there's our Friend: Beautiful. Spotless. Capable. Wonderful. Able to always counsel us. Almighty. How can He want to be with *us*?

Our relationship only works because Jesus knows how to lovingly deal with our sinfulness. Over and over He treats us as His friends. When we are misled, make poor choices, or retreat into unbelief, Jesus still upholds our dignity. He is able to convict our behavior without assassinating our character. He never sacrifices being loving for the sake of being right.

How different this is from how Satan would treat us. Instead of giving us grace, he wishes to disgrace us. Satan's desire is for us to feel disapproved, disowned, and discarded.

But not our wonderful friend, Jesus! No matter how marred or buried His image in us seems, Jesus still sees Himself in us. Underneath our woeful behavior, He sees beauty—beauty that He refuses to give up on until it is shined and polished and made perfect like Himself.

Your perfect friend believes in what He put in you. Such love is so far beyond words that all we can say is: "Isn't He wonderful?"

For to us a child is born, to us a son is given, and the government will be on his shoulders. And he will be called Wonderful Counselor, Mighty God, Everlasting Father, Prince of Peace.

ISAIAH 9:6

PRAYER

Express your gratitude for having a Savior who treats you with such dignity. Soak in His love for you until the image He sees becomes your vision, too.

BE GLORIFIED

Be glorified in the heavens,
Be glorified in the earth,
Be glorified in this temple,
Jesus, Jesus, be Thou glorified,
Jesus, Jesus, be Thou glorified.

—BILLY FUNK

God wants to prove His might in your life, especially when you feel weak. No kidding. So many people whom God used in Scripture were extraordinarily underqualified. Abraham, King Saul, Gideon, and the disciples all could have asked, "Who, me?" God certainly didn't choose them for their greatness. No, He chose them to glorify Himself.

If you want God to be glorified in your life, you may as well know that it probably will happen through your emptiness, weakness, and inability. Whenever God wants to really impress people, He begins with an impossibility—like creating a world out of nothing, having a virgin get pregnant, or bringing a crucified man back to life. Those are His favorite projects!

God is looking for people who feel as though they have nothing great to bring to the table. His only qualification is for them to say yes to whatever He asks.

Do you believe in God's goodness and power? Do you believe He can use all your unanswered questions and limited resources to produce something wonderful? Then pray the prayer that God loves to answer: Be glorified. When the impossible happens, people will know that God is at work again!

But he said to me, "My grace is sufficient for you, for my power is made perfect in weakness." Therefore I will boast all the more gladly about my weaknesses, so that Christ's power may rest on me.

2 CORINTHIANS 12:9

PRAYER

Don't just give Jesus all you have, give Him all you lack, too. Allow Him to use all you *can't* do and all you *don't* have to glorify Him.

M O R E   O F   Y O U R   G L O R Y

More of Your glory,
More of Your power,
More of Your Spirit in me,
Speak to my heart
And change my life;
Manifest Yourself in me.

It's been a long time
You have stayed on my mind.
There's a stirring in my soul,
And it causes me to know
How much I need You.

Send Your glory,
Send Your power,
Send Your Spirit—
Come and change me.

—LINDELL COOLEY AND BRUCE HAYNES

138

God has an interesting way of handling trouble. When life is most difficult, He reveals His glory. Often it is difficulty that causes a stirring in our souls, a stirring that causes us to know how much we need Him.

A week before the Transfiguration, Jesus had told His disciples clearly that He would be killed (Matthew 16:21-28). Imagine their heartache. All their hopes seemed lost. Then in one memorable moment, their suffering Savior changed into dazzling glory: "There he was transfigured before them. His face shone like the sun, and his clothes became as white as the light" (Matthew 17:2). All their doubts and fears crumbled into dust.

How we need God's glory in our troubled lives! How we need the stirring of our souls to cause us to cry out for more of His glory, more of His power, more of His Spirit in us.

God's glory provides all the hope, strength, and perspective we need to press on. His glory renews our assurance that God will be enough. It reminds us that one day our tragedies will be swallowed up in triumph. And it diminishes our present troubles as compared to the "eternal glory that far outweighs them all" (2 Corinthians 4:17).

Life is difficult, so ask God to speak to your heart, to change your life, to manifest Himself in you. He rewards such trust with a revelation of His glory.

His divine power has given us everything we need for life and godliness through our knowledge of him who called us by his own glory and goodness.

2 PETER 1:3

PRAYER

What do you need? More power? More love? More truth? Fix your eyes on Jesus and ask Him to reveal that aspect of His character to you. Then press on, believing He will.

SHOW ME YOUR WAYS

Show me Your ways that I may walk with You.
Show me Your ways, I put my hope in You.
The cry of my heart is to love You more,
To live with the touch of Your hand,
Stronger each day, show me Your ways.

—RUSSELL FRAGAR

Have you ever stared at one of those jumbled images of colored dots long enough to see the three-dimensional picture underneath? What a parallel to life. We can become so busy that our days seem like fragmented dots. Unless we stop long enough to ask God to show us His ways, we miss the real picture. That takes time. It takes that unique blend of concentration and relaxation as we pray: "Show me Your ways."

God will answer by giving us a perspective. Instead of seeing an opportunity to get ahead, we will see a chance to treat others right. Instead of seeing an unreasonable person, we will see the deeper image of hurt and want. Instead of focusing on our rights, we will see a chance to dispel strife. Instead of looking for ways to impress others, we will see what we can learn from them.

What a difference God's perspective makes! Every time we choose His way over our own, not only do we find meaning and purpose, but we also find the joy of life with God. Walking with Him is the best reward of all. God always has a way. You don't have to guess to figure it out. Step back from the fragmented pieces of your life and ask Him to show you. Soon you'll see it, too.

Show me your ways, O LORD, teach me your paths; guide me in your truth and teach me, for you are God my Savior, and my hope is in you all day long.

PSALM 25:4, 5

PRAYER

Take a few minutes to consider your upcoming activities. Ask God to show you how He sees them. Open your heart to hearing His purposes and perspective, and cooperate with Him.

M E E T   U S   H E R E

Meet us here,

Meet us here, Lord.

We are few, but we are strong

When You surround us.

Meet us here,

Meet us here, Lord.

As we gather in Your name,

Meet us here.

—DAN MARKS

What makes a church service powerful? Is it the amount of planning and preparation? Is it the quality of the music or preaching? Is it the obedience of the listeners? While all of these items are important, they only add up to a pile of dead works if God doesn't show up. We can sing, pray, and lift our hands, but apart from God, we will just be making religious motions. Worship is meaningless without the Lord. Once we know how desperate we are without Him, we pray, "Meet us here!"

Christ's powerful presence cuts through our confusion and breaks our bondages. His Spirit overcomes our sinfulness and fills us with peace. He restores our souls. The Bible tells us that when we gather in His name, He is right there with us.

You can't make your heart right, but He can. You don't know what you'll need for the days ahead, but He does. You can't have victory over Satan's attacks, but He can. You don't know God's mind, but He does. The Lord meets you with arms full of everything you need. He so much wants to help you! His dream is to live with you, walk with you, be your God, and make you thoroughly His.

God can do it! Ask Him to meet you right where you are.

For where two or three come together in my name, there am I with them.

MATTHEW 18:20

PRAYER

Ask God to meet you. Pray for Him to answer your every "I can't" with His "I can."

L O R D ,   Y O U   H A V E
M Y   H E A R T

Lord, You have my heart,

And I will search for Yours.

Jesus, take my life and lead me on.

Lord, You have my heart,

And I will search for Yours.

Let me be to You a sacrifice.

—M A R T I N   S M I T H

I f God has ever gotten a hold on your heart, you know how desperately you want to keep Him close. Thoughts of breaking fellowship seem ridiculous. We'd rather give up our sin than endanger our intimacy. Such a heart-to-heart relationship with God is the only thing that empowers us to say, "Let me be to You a sacrifice."

One of the most difficult things to sacrifice is our desire for a pain-free life. We're all too aware that to love is to risk being injured. Yet Jesus risks this all the time. He loves and pursues us even though we regularly let Him down. He continues to be jealous of our affection even though we give it to many lesser gods. His heart breaks when we refuse to learn the lessons He has for us! Yet, His love for us is unquenchable.

Could Christ really ask us to love each other this same way? It's uncomfortable to love those who criticize us, bless those who persecute us, and pray for those who hurt us. But compare it to the alternative: Either we suffer a little now as we die to ourselves and enjoy a pain-free eternity, or we live solely to enjoy this life and suffer a pain-filled eternity.

God lets us choose our pain! Our small sacrifices now will one day lead us into His everlasting arms. Together, forever, He will hold your heart. That makes it all worth it!

And so, dear brothers and sisters, I plead with you to give your bodies to God. Let them be a living and holy sacrifice—the kind he will accept. When you think of what he has done for you, is this too much to ask?

ROMANS 12:1

PRAYER

Don't let Jesus waste His love on you. Open your heart to let Jesus heal and cleanse you.

C O M E   I N T O   T H E
K I N G ' S   C H A M B E R S

O come into the King's chambers
And worship before His throne.
O come into the King's chambers
And His glory shall be shown . . .
O come into the King's chambers,
You will never be the same.

—DANIEL GARDNER

God has a plan for your life and it includes everything you're facing today. He knows what He's trying to work in you. He knows what He wants to do through you. Not a detail of your life has been left out. He plans to use it all for good.

Where do you learn this plan? In the king's chambers. The outer courts are where the crowds gather for praise, but in the inner room, lovers share their secrets. They express complete devotion, utter vulnerability, and genuine intimacy.

Your king wants to meet the requests you've been too afraid to even acknowledge. He wants to heal the wounds you've been too ashamed to mention. He wants to assure you that you cannot ask for too much of what is right and good and true. All the world's resources are His to share. Every opportunity comes from His divine arrangement. Your king is free to do as He sees best.

Are you discontent living in the outer courts? You would not long to go deeper if there wasn't something more. So quiet your heart. Learn to listen. Enter His chambers and let Him knit your soul together with His.

"For I know the plans I have for you," declares the LORD, "plans to prosper you and not to harm you, plans to give you hope and a future."

JEREMIAH 29:11

PRAYER

Ask God to look inside and show you what He sees. As you tune in to what He wants to do in your own heart, you'll begin to follow His plans.

PSALM 5 (GIVE EAR TO MY WORDS)

Give ear to my words, O Lord,

Consider my meditation.

Hearken unto the voice of my cry,

My King, and my God;

For unto Thee will I pray.

My voice shalt Thou hear

In the morning,

O Lord; in the morning

Will I direct my prayer

Unto Thee, and will look up.

—BILL SPROUSE JR.

Where would we be without our heavenly Friend to listen to us? When there's no one around to talk to, He hears. When no one else would understand, He will. When no one else cares, He does. Like the psalm writer, we can cry out to Him and know that He considers our silent meditations and hears the words that we cry.

Although any time is the right time to be with God, Psalm 5 mentions coming to God in the morning. It's a good time to evaluate the events of the previous day and to prepare for the new day. In the morning, our mind is fresh to process the thoughts God wants to give us. We might cry out for hope and let God build our expectation of His goodness. Or we might express our need for love and let God point out the obstacles we need to overcome, like how we long for an apology more than we long to forgive. Whatever our felt need, we can tell God about it and listen for His answer.

Living through a day without first receiving God's mercy is a lot like trying to make it until dinner without eating. We have to deal with the constant distraction of emptiness demanding to be filled. God's grace is ready to give us everything we need if we'll spend the time to receive it. He doesn't want us to run on empty for even a minute.

In the morning, O LORD, you hear my voice; in the morning I lay my requests before you and wait in expectation.

PSALM 5:3

PRAYER

How would you fill in this blank? "If I don't fit in anything else into my day, I want to fit in _____." If your answer was God, tell Him. He delights to have His children put Him first.

S P I R I T   S O N G

Jesus, oh Jesus,
Come and fill Your lambs.
Jesus, oh Jesus,
Come and fill Your lambs.

Oh let the Son of God enfold you
With His Spirit and His love.
Let Him fill your heart
And satisfy your soul.
Oh let Him have the things that hold you,
And His Spirit like a dove
Will descend upon your life
And make you whole.

—JOHN WIMBER

Knowing what's right usually isn't our problem. Doing it is. We know we should keep our mouth shut instead of demanding our rights and give up control instead of retaliating, but that's more than we can muster on our own. Thankfully, Jesus wants to fill us with His life. As we lean on Him, the perfect Lamb of God, we become lamb-like as well.

Isaiah 53:7 says that Jesus "was oppressed and afflicted, yet he did not open his mouth; he was led like a lamb to the slaughter, and as a sheep before her shearers is silent, so he did not open his mouth." Jesus knew when defending Himself was not part of God's plan. Despite His pain, He resisted the temptation to make events go His way. He didn't run over people's right to choose, even when they chose to act like the devil himself. Nothing evil was able to change Him from being a forgiving, caring person.

He wants to fill us with these same lamb-like qualities. It doesn't mean that we should sit back and let whatever happens, happen. We're responsible to ask, seek, and knock. When God answers with His plan, we can trust that He will give us what we need to cooperate with it.

Sometimes God needs to defend us. At other times, we have to let others feel the consequences of their sin before they will realize the truth. And at times, God needs to judge and settle the score. It's more than we can do, but not too much for our lamb-like Savior who lives in us. As He fills us, He supplies all we need to be forgiving, caring people.

The next day John saw Jesus coming toward him and said, "Look, the Lamb of God, who takes away the sin of the world!"
JOHN 1:29

PRAYER

Give up your right to anything God doesn't want you to have or be. It will make room in your heart for more of Jesus.

I W A N T T O B E
W H E R E Y O U A R E

I just want to be where You are,
Dwelling daily in Your presence.
I don't want to worship from afar;
Draw me near to where You are.

I just want to be where You are,
In Your dwelling place forever.
Take me to the place where You are;
I just want to be with You.

—DON MOEN

ome days don't you just hate for your quiet time to end? Wouldn't it be great if you could keep that heightened awareness of God's presence with you all day? When you feel like that, what you're really longing for is heaven.

We'll never be fully at peace until we're in our true home. Some days we long for it more than others. When we're weary from life's struggles, we want to go where God reigns supreme, where everyone and everything obeys His will perfectly, where we're known and loved completely.

But the best thing about heaven will be our reunion with the One we love. God's glory in all its fullness will completely penetrate and transform us. He will satisfy every longing we ever had. We'll be with the Creator, Sustainer, and Source of all joy. It's so wonderful that the Scripture writer could only say: "No eye has seen, no ear has heard, and no mind has imagined what God has prepared for those who love him" (1 Corinthians 2:9, NLT).

One day we won't be asking God to do anything for us or give anything to us because we'll have it all. We'll have Him! Until then, we echo the song: "I just want to be where You are, dwelling daily in Your presence."

One thing I ask of the LORD, this is what I seek: that I may dwell in the house of the LORD all the days of my life.

PSALM 27:4

PRAYER

Say to the Lord, "I just want to be with You." Imagine His delight as you tell Him how you long to be with Him.

I   O F F E R   M Y   L I F E

All that I am, all that I have,
I lay them down before You, O Lord.
All my regrets, all my acclaim,
The joy and the pain,
I'm making them Yours.

Lord, I offer my life to You,
Everything I've been through—
Use it for Your glory.

—DON MOEN AND CLAIRE CLONINGER

God never wastes our pain. It doesn't matter whether you brought it on yourself or it was inflicted on you. God doesn't compartmentalize your life into usable and unusable experiences. He will use it all for His glory if you'll let Him.

The events and actions that may have hurt you the most can speak the loudest to a hurting world. Lost people hunger for someone who understands their woundedness. They need to know those who wrestle with nagging questions and who don't get instant relief. Christians still fall down and get lost. Believers don't have it all together.

Christians who are transparent enough to admit they've been bumped and bruised by life will change the world. When we give up trying to impress people with our perfect image, God's grace shines through.

All that you are, all that you have, all your regrets, all your acclaim, all the joy, and all the pain. Lay these things before God to let Him use for His glory. What have you experienced that showed that God's grace was strong enough to sustain you, pursue you, and even use you? You may never understand why God allowed your pain, but you can be sure that as you tell the world of God's grace, He will get the glory.

Though I walk in the midst of trouble, you preserve my life; you stretch out your hand against the anger of my foes, with your right hand you save me.

PSALM 138:7

PRAYER

What difficulties are you facing today? God can take your hurts, disappointments, and imperfections and speak through them. Offer them to Him today.

LORD BE GLORIFIED

In my life, Lord,
Be glorified, be glorified.
In my life, Lord,
Be glorified today.

In my song, Lord,
Be glorified, be glorified.
In my song, Lord,
Be glorified today.

In your Church, Lord,
Be glorified, be glorified.
In your church, Lord,
Be glorified today.

—BOB KILPATRICK

How much do you want to see God glorified? If it's only just a little, then play it safe, and only do those things you're sure you can in your own strength. But if you want to see God glorified a lot, then follow Him to places where you'll need Him to be your indispensable necessity.

God is always up to something new, and He invites you to join Him. Whether it's a new career, a new ministry, a new relationship, or a new act of obedience, He wants you to take risks outside your comfort zone. His ideas of what He can do in and through you are so much bigger than your own, you'll have to stretch to grasp them.

Each time you step out in faith you'll move closer to the next challenge, and the next, and the next until you live in a way that depends on God every moment. Such a life brings God much glory!

So, how much are you willing to need God? And how much do you believe He can do? He loves to use the simple things to confound the wise, the weak things to shame the strong, and the lowly things to overcome the great. Follow His call as you pray for Him to be glorified in your life today and every day.

And whatever you ask in My name, that I will do, that the Father may be glorified in the Son.
JOHN 14:13 (NKJV)

PRAYER

It's often difficult to tell whether the call we're hearing is from God or our own ego. Let the Holy Spirit examine your motivations to clarify whether you are hearing something that needs heeding or something that needs healing.

SANCTUARY

Lord, prepare me to be a sanctuary—
Pure and holy, tried and true.
With thanksgiving I'll be a living
Sanctuary for You.

—JOHN THOMPSON AND RANDY SCRUGGS

ave you ever looked so hard for God in your life that you forgot He was right there—inside you? Maybe you were so intent on finding His purpose or knowing His will that you missed the fact that all day He was giving you ideas, whispering He loved you, and encouraging you to keep going.

You're not alone. Paul had to remind the church at Corinth that they were temples of the Holy Spirit if Christ had come to live in them (1 Corinthians 6:19). If he were writing today, Paul might call them sanctuaries. Just as this song says, "With thanksgiving I'll be a living sanctuary for You."

As a sanctuary, God wants us to be a safe place for others to come in order to experience His love. He wants us to be a refuge for souls who are hurting and a strong arm for those who have been burdened. No, we don't have to work miracles; we just have to connect people with the Miracle-worker. As we relinquish our role to Him, our lives become a holy place for others.

The life of Jesus in you may be the only sanctuary some people ever enter. Believe in that life and nourish it through prayer and Scripture. Then the God who lives in you will welcome others to know Him, too.

Do you not know that your body is a temple of the Holy Spirit, who is in you, whom you have received from God? You are not your own; you were bought at a price. Therefore honor God with your body.
1 CORINTHIANS 6:19, 20

PRAYER

How pure and holy is your sanctuary? Ask God to clean out the things that distract you from Him. Receive His grace so your life will be a safe place for others.

No Other Name

His name is exalted
Far above the earth.
His name is high
Above the heavens.
His name is exalted
Far above the earth.
Give glory and honor
And praise unto His name.

—Robert Gay

D o you believe that Jesus rules over the universe? Even more crucial, do you believe He rules over your life—your past, your present, and your future? Before your story ever began, He knew it beginning to end. He has only allowed in it the people He created. He has only let happen the events He already knew He would use for your good. Nothing in your life has taken the Lord by surprise.

In His supreme sovereignty, Jesus understands everything inside you. He knows all your motivations, feelings, thoughts, immaturities, hidden faults, and hindrances. You are no surprise to Him. He has never said, "If only I'd known better, I would have changed that." He's always known it all!

If you wrestle with what might have been, exalt Jesus to His proper place. The Creator and Ruler always knew what would be. Nothing has happened by accident. You're in this place and time by His design. You may be on the speck marked "here." He is there, too, reigning supremely over it all.

But our High Priest offered himself to God as one sacrifice for sins, good for all time. Then he sat down at the place of highest honor at God's right hand.

HEBREWS 10:12 (NLT)

PRAYER

Ask God to help you let go of all that "should have been" and accept His exalted rule over your life.

M O R E   L O V E ,   M O R E   P O W E R

More love, more power,
More of You in my life.
More love, more power,
More of You in my life.

And I will worship You
With all of my heart,
And I will worship You
With all of my mind,
And I will worship You
With all of my strength,
For You are my Lord.

—JUDE DEL HIERRO

lose athletic contests are exciting for fans and players. Good athletes enjoy playing against someone who is an even match. Rivals challenge us to reach for every ounce of skill and power we posses. They push us to new levels in our game.

The same is true in our spiritual lives. Few of us would volunteer for a mission that required us to struggle daily for a higher level of love and power. But since our enemy is great, we're required to press for more. In fact, thanks in part to Satan's challenges, we can know great victory. What joy would there be in overcoming a weak enemy?

Relying on ourselves, we'd never overcome such a formidable foe. But as we let go of all that defeats us, we make more room for Christ to fill us. He replaces our unforgiveness, regrets, and doubts with His love, peace, and power as we worship Him. There's no limit to what we can receive, because there's always more of Him to have.

In the end, it's really no contest, because the One who lives in us is greater than the one who lives in the world. Ever since the Cross, Satan has been doomed to defeat. His advances will only serve to bring us into new levels of God's love and power.

You, dear children, are from God and have overcome them, because the one who is in you is greater than the one who is in the world.

1 JOHN 4:4

PRAYER

If you really want victory in your life, you first have to join the winning side. Dedicate all your heart, mind, and strength to God's glory. Then let Him fill you with all you need to overcome your enemy.

I GIVE YOU MY HEART

Lord, I give You my heart,
I give You my soul,
I live for You alone.
Every breath that I take,
Every moment I'm awake,
Lord, have Your way in me.

—REUBEN MORGAN

How badly do you want to be free in Christ? It usually takes getting fed up with the world's empty promises, tired of Satan's traps, or sick of our own stupid reactions before we really want to be free. Until that point, we stay bound by our stray affections.

Satan deceives us into thinking that we should only give God part of our heart, as if that way we could get the best of both worlds: our own selfishness and God's goodness. The truth is that the very thing we refuse to surrender imprisons us. We never experience the freedom of walking with God and enjoying His presence until we let go.

If God is trying to wrestle you to the ground to give in, know that whatever you let go of is nothing compared to knowing Him. His love and peace are so much more real, more stable, and more lasting; you won't believe you didn't give in sooner.

God always finds more for us to surrender—hidden attachments and unhealthy desires. By giving them all to Him, they lose their power to control us. Little by little He sets us free to love and worship Him. That's a freedom worth surrendering for.

Blessed are they who keep his statutes and seek him with all their heart.

PSALM 119:2

PRAYER

Ask God to show you what you may be hanging on to instead of Him. Then ask for the faith in His goodness, power, and love to be able to give it up and be set free.

MAKE ME A SERVANT

Make me a servant,
Humble and meek.
Lord, let me lift up
Those who are weak.
And may the prayer
Of my heart always be,
Make me a servant,
Make me a servant,
Make me a servant today.

—KELLY WILLARD

Throughout the Bible, we read of God's choosing humble servants to convey His power. Where would Naaman be without his wife's servant girl sending him to Elisha to be healed? Where would Jesus be without Mary accepting God's will as the handmaiden of the Lord? Where would the Christian church be without Paul and Timothy? Where would we be without Jesus, the One who came to serve and give His life as a ransom for many?

These servants, and countless others like them, humbled themselves in order to serve. Their lives didn't revolve around developing their spiritual gifts, finding something great to do for God, or even becoming the best they could be. Instead they asked: Who can I help? What can I do to fit in with God's plan? What need is God calling me to meet? How can I obey? As a result, they changed the world.

Your humble service can do the same. Trust that whatever God has put in you He can work powerfully through. Whatever your gift, use it to serve others. Then people will hear the powerful message of God's grace: They are worth being loved.

For even the Son of Man did not come to be served, but to serve, and to give his life as a ransom for many.

MARK 10:45

PRAYER

Ask God to examine what holds you back from serving others.

C R E A T E   I N   M E

Create in me a clean heart, oh God,
That I might serve You.
Create in me a clean heart, oh God,
That I might be renewed.
So fill me and heal me,
And bring me back to You.
Create in me a clean heart, oh God,
That I might serve You.

— MARY RICE HOPKINS

How good is your vision? Your eyes may be 20/20, but spiritually we see with our hearts. That's why Paul's prayer for the church at Ephesus was that "the eyes of your heart may be enlightened" (Ephesians 1:18). Are you seeing God as clearly as you'd like?

When our hearts are dirty, our vision is impaired. Like this songwriter, we need God to come and clean us.

Sometimes we aren't seeing God in our lives, and we don't even know where we're "off." We just know something's not right. That's when it's helpful to pray some questions and ask the Holy Spirit to do some probing. "How have I been resisting what You've been trying to teach me?" "Is there something true about You, God, that I haven't been believing?" As we open the door, the Holy Spirit reveals our sin and is able to remove any detriments to our vision.

God is always at work (John 5:17). He wants you to know Him better and better. He longs for you to see how much He loves and cares for you. He wants what's best for you and is working to bring you into all of it. If you can't see that, it may be time to pray the words of the song and let God clean out your heart.

Create in me a clean heart, O God; and renew a right spirit within me.

PSALM 51:10 (KJV)

PRAYER

A clean heart can have a powerful effect on the world. Don't try to rush God into using you before He's done what He needs to in your heart.

REFINER'S FIRE

Purify my heart,
Cleanse me from my sin
And make me holy.
Purify my heart,
Cleanse me from my sin
Deep within.

Refiner's fire, my heart's one desire
Is to be holy, set apart for You, Lord.
I choose to be holy, set apart for You,
my Master,
Ready to do Your will.

—BRIAN DOERKSEN

It's humbling to read Luke's introduction to his story about the Pharisee and the tax collector who went to the temple to pray (Luke 18:9-14). Luke says that Jesus told the parable "to some who were confident of their own righteousness and looked down on everybody else." In other words, "Listen up all of you who focus on doing all the right things but miss how off you really are."

That was the Pharisee's problem. He was so busy tithing and sacrificing that he was blind to the judgmental attitude of his heart. In his self-righteousness, he missed God's desire for him to receive mercy and then pass it on to others.

When we focus on our outward actions, especially how we compare to others who act worse, we, too, are in danger of missing the depth of sin in our own hearts. That's where God wants to do His major work. As we let Him examine our desires and attitudes, our righteousness is revealed for what it is—a flimsy substitute for confidence in God's mercy.

You can trust God's love and kindness toward you. He sits like a refiner of silver, closely watching over you as He purifies you. When the "dross" is burned away, what is left is a beautiful piece of silver in which the Refiner can see His reflection. The process may be painful at times, but God is cleansing you so that He can see His reflection in you.

He will sit and judge like a refiner of silver, watching closely as the dross is burned away.

MALACHI 3:3 (NLT)

PRAYER

Unless God reveals the sins in our hearts, we'll probably never see them. Let Him examine your attitudes. Remember, the fire of His love is strong enough to purge any sin.

WE ARE AN OFFERING

All that we have,
All that we are,
All that we hope to be,
We give to You,
We give to You.

—DWIGHT LILES

an God be trusted? Is He really as good as He says He is?
Since the Garden of Eden, people have wrestled with these questions. We know we should surrender wholeheartedly to Him, but doubts tempt us to withdraw, trust ourselves, and take no risks.

We will never know anyone more deserving of our surrender. *God promises to give us all good things:* "He who did not spare his own Son, but gave him up for us all—how will he not also, along with him, graciously give us all things?" (Romans 8:32).

God promises to be faithful, even when we're faithless: "If we are faithless, he will remain faithful" (2 Timothy 2:13).

God promises to never abandon us: "Never will I leave you; never will I forsake you" (Hebrews 13:5).

God promises to give us peace no one can take away: "I have told you these things, so that in me you may have peace" (John 16:33a).

God promises to take us home to be with Him: "I am going there to prepare a place for you. I will come back and take you to be with me that you also may be where I am" (John 14:2, 3).

Give Him complete control. You'll find Him completely trustworthy.

Offer yourselves to God, as those who have been brought from death to life; and offer the parts of your body to him as instruments of righteousness.

ROMANS 6:13b

PRAYER

Ask God to reveal the fears that hold you back from surrendering to Him. Examine them in light of His trustworthiness.

A L L   I   O N C E   H E L D   D E A R
(K N O W I N G   Y O U)

Knowing You, Jesus, knowing You,
There is no greater thing.
You're my all, You're the best,
You're my joy, my righteousness,
And I love You, Lord.

—GRAHAM KENDRICK

We spend so much time and effort trying to know what we cannot know: what trials lie ahead; how our children will turn out; what God might do through us. Thankfully, the secret of getting ahead in the spiritual life isn't what we know but *whom* we know.

When we let go of all we cannot figure out, we get to know God. That's not an accident. God planned life to work that way. Instead of pursuing Him, we can easily slip into pursuing answers or his plans. But when we do that, our intimacy always suffers.

God reveals Himself to those who put Him first. He entrusts His plans to us (Psalm 25:14) and graciously imparts Himself to us when we want to know Him more than anything. His goal is to draw us into a relationship so strong that we'll trust Him even without the answers.

If you've been frustrated by God's silence, it could be that you're asking the wrong questions. As hard as it is, let go of needing to know anything besides Him. (Even if that means knowing you're loved or knowing God's will). Make needing to know God your only pursuit. He will not keep you clueless as to the rest. It's just that He never wants you to forget that it's all about a relationship with Him.

Continue your love to those who know you, your righteousness to the upright in heart.

PSALM 36:10

PRAYER

The apostle Paul considered everything a loss compared to the surpassing greatness of knowing Christ Jesus (Philippians 3:8). Set aside your other pressing needs in prayer today and pursue knowing Him.

HE IS ABLE

He is able, more than able,
To accomplish what concerns me today.
He is able, more than able,
To handle anything that comes my way.
He is able, more than able,
To do much more than I could ever dream.
He is able, more than able,
To make me what He wants me to be.

—RORY NOLAND AND GREG FERGUSON

What relief this song brings! We don't have to handle it all! We don't have to be consumed with our problems as if it's all depending on us. Knowing God can handle our concerns frees us to live balanced lives.

God wants us to experience rest and play as much as He wants us to work hard. Jesus came that we might have and enjoy our lives (John 10:10) and not be bound by anxiety or dread. As much as we'd like it, we don't have to know the answers to these questions: Where will God lead me? How will He resolve this? When will I get relief?

Relief comes when we're content to live the questions. When we embrace just the step in front of us, we can revel in the anticipation of what God will do with all the rest. Whatever lies ahead will be good, because God will be there and He is always good. He always gives us what we need.

God is preparing your circumstances so that everyone who sees you will acknowledge that you are a person whom the Lord has blessed (Isaiah 61:9). It's your inheritance as God's child. Jesus died to give it to you. Receive it. Live the questions and let God accomplish the rest.

Cast all your anxiety on him because he cares for you.

1 PETER 5:7

PRAYER

Sometimes we get so concerned with the future, we miss the step right in front of us God wants us to take. Tell God everything that concerns you, put it in His hands, and then live as if you are in His will. Ask Him for the faith to believe He is guiding your steps, even when you don't have all the answers that you would like.

HERE I AM, LORD

Here I am, Lord,

It is I, Lord.

I have heard You calling in the night.

I will go, Lord,

If You lead me.

I will hold Your people in my heart.

—DANIEL L SCHUTTE

When God needed a faithful leader for Israel, He called Samuel. And He literally *called*. "The LORD came and stood there, calling as at the other times, 'Samuel! Samuel!' Then Samuel said, 'Speak, for your servant is listening' " (1 Samuel 3:10). When He needed a prophet for Israel, Isaiah answered the call, "Then I heard the voice of the Lord saying, 'Whom shall I send? And who will go for us?' And I said, 'Here am I. Send me!' " (Isaiah 6:8).

God may not call you to serve Him as clearly as He did Samuel or Isaiah. Instead, He may call in a more quiet, but no less certain way. However it's packaged, God is calling you to love people the way He does. Where do we get the power to love people who may wound us, offend us, or not deserve it in our minds? Only by seeing them as broken, blind, and in need of a Savior—at exactly the same place we would be if Jesus hadn't rescued us. Jesus' love never forgets that this is what we are. He doesn't expect perfection. He isn't surprised when we fail. He knows we would be empty if He didn't fill us, broken if He didn't heal us, and alone if He didn't belong to us.

That's the message He asks us to share with others. He's calling you. How will you respond?

A new command I give you: Love one another. As I have loved you, so you must love one another.

JOHN 13:34

PRAYER

Is God's call clear in your life? If not, ask Him to put his desires on your heart. As you step out, you'll find out what He wants.

179

G I V E   T H A N K S

Give thanks with a grateful heart,
Give thanks to the Holy One,
Give thanks because He's given
Jesus Christ His Son.

And now, let the weak say, "I am strong,"
Let the poor say, "I am rich,
Because of what
The Lord has done for us."
Give thanks.

—HENRY SMITH

Human-made religions center on what people can do for their god. But Christianity centers on what God has done for us. He gives us His Son, as a continual source of comfort and freedom, even when we have nothing to offer in return. To receive Him, we only need to let go of trying to save ourselves and rely on Him alone to save us.

This requires admitting our weaknesses and allowing God to use them to show Himself strong. That's humbling! And oh how we fight it. We want to be loved for being so good, not for being so needy. Yet God knows this is exactly what we are. Instead of being put off by our inabilities, He encourages us to come to Him. He knows that only people who have come to the end of themselves rely on Him. God has a limitless supply of hope and strength for people who recognize their need. No matter how "poor" we may feel, we are the richest people in the world, all because of what the Lord has done for us. For this, we give thanks.

He gives strength to the weary and increases the power of the weak.

ISAIAH 40:29

PRAYER

Give thanks to God for all He has done for you. Invite Him to show Himself strong in a difficult situation, and thank Him for the opportunity to rely on Him.

PERMISSIONS

"All Hail King Jesus" by David Moody. ©1980 Dayspring Music/BMI (ASCAP). Used by permission.

"All I Once Held Dear (Knowing You)" by Graham Kendrick. ©1993 Make Way Music (admin. by Music Services)/ASCAP. Used by permission.

"As The Deer" by Martin Nystrom. ©1984 Maranatha! Praise, Inc. (admin. by The Copyright Company, Nashville, TN)/ASCAP. Used by permission.

"Awesome God" by Rich Mullins. ©1988 BMG Songs, Inc./ASCAP. Used by permission.

"Be Exalted O God" by Brent Chambers. ©1977 Scripture In Song (a division of Integrity Music/ASCAP. All rights reserved. Used by permission.

"Be Glorified" by Billy Funk. ©1991 Integrity's Hosanna! Music/ASCAP. All rights reserved. Used by permission.

"Blessed Be The Lord God Almighty" by Bob Fitts. ©1984 Integrity's Hosanna! Music/ASCAP. All rights reserved. Used by permission.

"Blessed Be The Name Of The Lord" by Don Moen. ©1986 Integrity's Hosanna! Music/ASCAP. All rights reserved. Used by permission.

"Celebrate Jesus" by Gary Oliver. ©1988 Integrity's Hosanna! Music/ASCAP. All rights reserved. Used by permission.

"Change My Heart, Oh God" by Eddie Espinosa. ©1982 Mercy/Vineyard Publishing/ASCAP. Used by permission.

"Come Into His Presence" by Lynn Baird. ©1988 Integrity's Hosanna! Music/ASCAP. All rights reserved. Used by permission.

"Come Into The King's Chambers" by Daniel Gardner. ©1981 Integrity's Hosanna! Music/ASCAP. All rights reserved. Used by permission.

"Come Let Us Adore Him / Thou Art Worthy" by Pauline Mills. ©1963 Fred Bock Music Company/ASCAP. Used by permission.

"Come Let Us Worship And Bow Down" by Dave Doherty. ©1980 Maranatha! Praise, Inc. (admin. by The Copyright Company, Nashville, TN)/ASCAP. Used by permission.

"Come Now Is The Time To Worship" by Brian Doerksen. ©1998 Vineyard Songs (UK/ERIE) (Admin. by Mercy/Vineyard Publishing)/ASCAP. Used by permission.

"Create In Me" by Mary Rice Hopkins. ©1989 Big Steps 4 U/Maranatha! Music (admin. by The Copyright Company, Nashville, TN)/ASCAP. Used by permission.

"Father, I Adore You" by Terrye Coelho Strom. ©1972 Maranatha! Praise, Inc. (admin. by The Copyright Company, Nashville, TN)/ASCAP. Used by permission.

"Give Thanks" by Henry Smith. ©1978 Integrity's Hosanna! Music/ASCAP. All rights reserved. Used by permission.

"Glorify Thy Name" by Donna Adkins. ©1976 Maranatha! Praise, Inc. (admin. by The Copyright Company, Nashville, TN)/ASCAP. Used by permission.

"God Will Make A Way" by Don Moen. ©1990 Integrity's Hosanna! Music/ASCAP. All rights reserved. Used by permission.

"He Has Made Me Glad" by Leona Von Brethorst. ©1976 Maranatha! Praise, Inc. (admin. by The Copyright Company, Nashville, TN)/ASCAP. Used by permission.

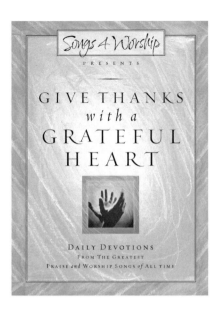

A beautiful, full-color daily devotional of thanksgiving and love toward God, Give Thanks with a Grateful Heart *features 90 more spiritually moving devotionals based on the greatest praise and worship songs of all time.*
ISBN 1-59145-022-5

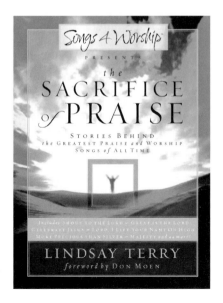

An inspiring companion volume, The Sacrifice of Praise *tells the fascinating stories behind the creation of the greatest praise and worship songs of all time.*
ISBN 1-59145-014-4

INTEGRITY
PUBLISHERS

Available wherever books are sold.